Fresh Every Morning

. . . And he said, "Say this to the people of Israel, 'I AM has sent me to you.' "

EXODUS 3:14

❧ FRESH ☙
EVERY MORNING
by Gerald Hamilton Kennedy

HARPER & ROW, PUBLISHERS

New York

Unless otherwise noted, all Scripture quotations
are from the Revised Standard Version.

LIBRARY OF CONGRESS CATALOG CARD NUMBER 66-15042

THIS IS FOR GEORGE HEIMRICH

Contents

	Preface	ix
1.	Dealing with the Eternal	1
2.	Always in Debt	12
3.	Fresh Every Morning	22
4.	Dwelling Place of Wonder	31
5.	If You Go with Us	41
6.	Treasure in Earthen Vessels	51
7.	In the Name of the Lord	61
8.	Concerning Peace of Mind	71
9.	I Can Leap Over a Wall	80
10.	Time for Decision	89
11.	God in the Narrow Places	99
12.	Sickness by the Pool	109
13.	Go Up, Take Possession	119
14.	One True Sentence	128
15.	Wake Up To Reality	137
16.	Do Not Be Afraid	146
17.	Four Books To Live By	156
18.	He Did Not Quit!	167
19.	There Came One Running	177
20.	One Witness in One World	186

Preface

MOSES HEARD the voice of God out of the burning bush and received the divine commission to bring the people out of Egypt.
But a practical question arose in his mind. How will they know
they ought to listen to me? What shall I say to them if they ask who
sent me? And God said, "Say this to the people of Israel, 'I AM has
sent me to you.'" This may have happened in the thirteenth century
before Jesus was born, but it has a contemporary sound to Christian
preachers thirty-two hundred years later.

What shall we say to the people? For we are called to address
them every week in the name of God and by His authority. The
task does not grow easier with the passing years, but harder. When
it is time to begin preparation for next Sunday's sermon, I run more
scared than ever.

These sermons have no single theme except they seem to me what
God demands ought to be said in our time. The Good News comes
from God through Christ by way of sinful men. We can only
confess our inadequacy and pray that the Holy Spirit will take our
poor, stumbling words and make of them what God wants said to
the people. I wish I could preach better, but I have never doubted
that preach I must. All the talk about poor preaching and the
advisability of eliminating it, or at the very least, minimizing it, does
not impress me. I have heard it all my life, and after more than
thirty years of preaching and appointing preachers to their pulpits,
the proclamation of the Word seems to me the chief essential of our
ministry.

I express thanks to the congregations large and small, urban and
rural, who listened first to what is in this book. I am a debtor to my
wife whose criticism is gentle but firm, and to my secretary Dorothy
Hancock who carries extra burdens with grace.

GERALD KENNEDY

Hollywood, California, 1966

Fresh Every Morning

❦ I ❧

Dealing with the Eternal

And David was afraid of the Lord that day. . . .
II SAMUEL 6:9

LET US look at one of the most difficult stories in the Old Testament and see if God is not speaking some word to us through it. After David had been made king and captured Jerusalem, he must bring the Ark up to the Holy City. The Ark was a chest in which the Law God gave to Moses was kept. So David and his men placed the sacred chest on a cart drawn by oxen, and, accompanied by a host of people singing and dancing, they started on the journey from the house of Abinadab to Jerusalem. It was a joyous occasion, a sort of triumphal procession. But at one place on the journey the oxen stumbled, and it looked as if the Ark would fall off the cart. A man named Uzzah, standing alongside, put out his hand to steady it and almost immediately he fell dead. The tragedy made a great impression upon people, and they said he must have been stricken by the Lord for putting his hand on the holy object.

Why should God kill a man for trying to hold the Ark steady and keep it from falling to the ground? The character of God is at stake. This story has been explained in different ways, and most scholars view it as merely a coincidence which the people wrongly ascribed to Uzzah's act and God's punishment. They believed that the object was holy, and that to touch a holy object even with the best of intentions was to invite death. Maybe Uzzah simply slipped and fell and the writer of the story jumped to the conclusion that it was because of something he had done.

To me this story is saying that there are some things which are not to be manipulated or interfered with by human beings. There are some things in life which are for us to adjust to and not for us to arrange to suit our wishes. Surely we are being told that not every reality is amendable to our desires and that if a generation assumes it has the right to arrange everything to its convenience, that generation will die. There are eternal truths which cannot be amended.

It is characteristic of us to assume that practically everything is to be decided by a majority vote. We are better able to determine public opinion than any generation before us. A democracy is committed to the rule by the will of the majority, and this leads to the conclusion that what the public wants, the public must have. One of the modern weaknesses is to assume that we can settle all issues by voting on them.

As I travel around the country I see a rather common newspaper feature. A reporter simply approaches persons at random and asks their opinions on some subject. Now if it is something that is merely a matter of opinion, such as the Dodgers' chances for winning the pennant or who is the most beautiful movie actress, that is one thing. But oftentimes these questions have to do with scientific fact, and people are invited to express their feelings as if it makes any difference at all how they feel about it. When you are dealing with facts, majority votes do not count and opinions are only of academic interest.

Or we may look at what I have labeled "the Kinsey psychology." When the Indiana University professor published his report on contemporary sex activities, a general feeling arose that if enough people were doing it, no guilt was attached. We are to believe, so the report seemed to assume, that if enough people agree that a certain activity is now acceptable, automatically it is no longer immoral. This is the belief raised in the old refrain "fifty million Frenchmen can't be wrong." There is nothing more false than to believe that, for not only fifty million Frenchmen, but a hundred million Frenchmen could be wrong.

We are anxious to hear what the public opinion polls tell us, especially if there is an election in the offing. This is fine if it merely indicates which party is ahead and where the weak spots of the campaign are to be found. But if we go on to assume that the majority opinion automatically decides the right and wrong of an issue, we are certainly confused. History shows too many times where the majority led a society over the abyss and where the truth was to be found in a minority report.

A city school teacher brought a rabbit to show the children. They were delighted with it and asked all kinds of questions. Finally, someone asked if it was a boy rabbit or a girl rabbit. The teacher was a little bit flustered and finally confessed that she did not know. Then one little girl said, "We could vote on it." This psychology characterizes so much of our modern life, and to this point of view the old story of Uzzah speaks with blunt, brutal truth. There are some things that do not depend on anybody's vote. Whether the majority is for them or against them has nothing to do with the case. There are some things not to be manipulated or adjusted.

In three crucial areas we must come to terms with this truth. The first is

Morality.

I believe in the moral law. I believe that God has established this law as unchangeable and as unmanipulatable as the law of gravity. I believe that the only choice we have is to discover what the law is and live by it or to ignore it and die by it.

All of my life I have been hearing about a "new morality." Every generation seems to assume that the moral principles of their fathers are old-fashioned and outgrown. Every new point of view assumes that some things formerly thought wrong are no longer wrong, and that we can act as if we live in a new moral climate. It is certainly true that some of the interpretations of morality and some of the customs we have established are outgrown and could be discarded.

But I do not believe there is any such thing as a new morality, and so far as morals are concerned, the same kind of behavior which brought the downfall of Greece or Rome will bring the downfall of America or Russia.

We are constantly under the demand to rethink our sex attitudes and our sex customs. Nothing seems more old-fashioned to the modern generation than the way their fathers and mothers courted and married. Some of the Victorian attitudes toward marriage fifty years ago are always good for hilarity and amusement. It is true, of course, that some of those things seem stilted, stuffy, and should be outgrown. Our children do take different attitudes toward one another, and in some ways their attitudes are a great improvement over those of the Puritans. As we change our styles of dress, we change our styles of courtship.

But essentially we cannot change anything about this terrible, wonderful gift God has given us. It is still true that rules operate, and if we follow them, sex becomes fulfillment and joy. If we ignore those laws, sex turns into lust and degradation. It is still true that no man can use a woman as a means to an end, nor can a woman use a man as a pawn to fulfill an ambition. The relationship between man and woman is something holy and unchangeable. When we forget this all of our sophistication and smartness becomes a mere cover for failure and defeat.

The family is deeply affected by its environment. Modern families live a different kind of life than our fathers knew. But the essential thing about the family has not changed, and what children learn from their parents and their homes is still the fundamental determinant of their future. Mothers may think they can turn their children over to housekeepers and have their own careers outside the home, but that does not work any better today than it did a thousand years ago. There are unchanging laws which govern the home and the family, and if in the name of being new and up-to-date we ignore those laws and break them, the only result is broken homes and delinquency.

When we look to the business world, we find things being done differently today. We have modern machines and modern methods of production, but underneath all of the machinery there is the necessity for truth and honesty. No society lasts very long if its business leaders are untrustworthy and cheat when they have the opportunity. That the citizens of a nation must have a fundamental trust in one another is one of those laws which must not be broken if we are to have a future.

The sacredness of a person represents an unchanging and eternal fact with which we must come to terms. Christianity taught this from the beginning, and there is no modern discovery which has made it out of date. Persons are final values in this world, and if we deny it, ill fares the land.

We look for something new in marriage and imply that no one should be shocked any longer by divorce. We can make fun of the old idea that a man and a woman stayed together when they were married even if they were unhappy. But the easy attitude we take does not lead us to life. When the marriage vows are broken easily and when the divorce rate increases to the extent that marriage becomes merely an experiment, there appear cracks in the walls and the foundations tremble. There is always something immoral about a trial marriage.

We obey the laws of righteousness in our society to save us from the jungle. Civilization depends upon justice and equity. It makes no difference whether it was Ananias lying about the disposal of his property or whether it is a Billy Sol Estes organizing a gigantic hoax on the government. Amos lived eight hundred years before Christ, and in unforgettable lines he described the demands of the moral law. He pronounced retribution on those who bought the poor for silver and the needy for a pair of shoes. The moral law demands, he said, that "justice roll down like waters, and righteousness like an ever-flowing stream." There is nothing new in that, and there is nothing changeable about it either.

I read not long ago that in Albuquerque, New Mexico, there is a street called Shangri-La Drive. But it is a dead-end street. For all those who think that morality is merely a matter of majority opinion, the outcome is always a dead end. In the name of being modern or changing some of these hard rules of life to suit our convenience, we find out when it is too late that we have reached out to manipulate a sacred value and we have been destroyed.

The second realm where we must not interfere is

Freedom.

Here there is a sense in which it is all or nothing, and the moment we begin to manipulate or limit, we have destroyed it.

Take, for example, censorship. Someone is always coming along with the very best of intentions to keep what they regard as the indecent from other people. A man reported that when he was a boy his maiden aunt had given him a Bible. Being concerned with its frankness in places, she had pasted certain pages together lest his boyish mind become corrupted. This, he reported, simply made the places easier to find. It reminded me of an experience when I was a student preacher in a Connecticut village. An elderly lady gave me several novels, and when I read them, I discovered that whenever she had come to a risqué passage, she simply cut it out. Of course, I had to find another book and read the missing sections.

Censorship seems to be so reasonable if it is being practiced by good people. We can hardly find objections to eliminating what to our mind ought to be eliminated. You can make a good case for the necessity of holding up standards of decency and making it un-lawful to print certain books and show certain pictures. If we could be sure that the censor was always a reasonable and responsible person, which is to say a person who thinks as we think, there would be little debate on the subject.

But the difficulty is that if it works for one side, it will work for the other. Supposing a Hitler comes to power and decides that some things are not good for the people to read. Suppose the tyrant wants to keep truth from the citizens of the nation. When the principle of censorship has been established, then there is no legitimate reason why, if used by one side, it cannot be used by the other. I am quite willing to accept censorship if I can be the censor, but I begin to ask questions about it if someone with whom I thoroughly disagree wants to do the censoring.

I have come to the conclusion finally that censorship is wrong and that it raises more questions than it solves. We have to raise the tastes of all men so that the filthy and the obscene will have no appeal. Freedom to read must be respected, and except in a very few extreme cases, we must insist on men's right to choose for themselves.

Or look at this principle in terms of ideas. Are there some ideas that are positively dangerous? Possibly. Are there some ideas that are disgusting? Of course. But who is to decide and who shall have the final word? In America during these past years we have been very foolish, or at least so it seems to me. We have been so afraid of communism that we have forbidden any serious mention of it or any objective study of it. We are afraid for our young people to hear anybody who is an avowed communist, and on this subject at least, we have exercised an extreme censorship. Indeed, a few years ago during the McCarthy era, if we had heard of any man who even so much as studied the Russian language, he would have been investigated.

This, I am sure, is a grievous and dangerous mistake. We have to believe in our way of life and its traditions enough to think that our young people have a basis of judgment of other systems. When a few Korean soldiers were brainwashed and defected, the fault was primarily ours. Why had these boys never had a chance to study what communism is and what its weaknesses and evils are? Why were they never prepared to fight bravely on the battlefield of ideas? Jesus said that the truth would make us free, and the only way men find truth is to be at liberty to investigate every idea.

Justice Oliver Wendell Holmes, Jr., in the Abrams case in 1919, wrote these words: "But when men have realized that time has upset many fighting faiths, they may come to believe even more than they believe the very foundations of their own conduct that the ultimate good desired is better reached by free trade in ideas—that the best test of truth is the power of the thought to get itself accepted in the competition of the market, and that truth is the only ground upon which their wishes safely can be carried out. That at any rate is the theory of our Constitution. It is an experiment, as all life is an experiment. Every year if not every day we have to wager our salvation upon some prophecy based upon imperfect knowledge." Words not to be forgotten!

The freedom of man is an idea that cannot be limited. South Africa has established its apartheid policy and determined to keep the black man in virtual slavery. I thought when I visited that unhappy land a few years ago, and I still think, that they are merely postponing a terrible day of judgment because all men will be free. In America we are discovering that the revolution of civil rights has been held off for a hundred years but that now it has arrived. The history of slavery is clear enough. You cannot demand freedom for yourself and deny it to your brother. The moment we censor it or limit it, we have destroyed it. Freedom is of a piece and it can never be divided.

In a town square in Kansas there is this sign: "No ball playing. No bicycle riding. No pets. Remember, this is your park!" We would like to make life subject to our limitations. But God has made man free, and we cannot interfere with this freedom or limit it lest we lose it for ourselves.

Now the third thing to be said is that we must apply this principle to

God.

John Newton wrote, "If you think you see the Ark of the Lord falling, you can be quite sure that it is due to a swimming in your own head." God is not someone to use, and it is for men to discover His will and yield themselves to it without compromise.

Let us understand clearly that we cannot manipulate God. There are some pseudo-Christian sects of our time which promise certain rewards if we learn how to use God for our benefit. There are some groups within Christianity itself which are guilty of this blasphemy. Indeed, to some extent our American religion falls into the trap of teaching people that God is one of those resources we can use for profit. We try to package Him and market Him.

Consider our attitude toward worship. We come to the conclusion that worship is merely a feeling we may build up by certain techniques. We conclude that to worship is to make ourselves feel better, and we use the church and God as a means of quieting our fears and increasing our happiness. Our hymns are too often subjective and become sentimental. The great hymns of the church are always objective and center our attention on God and His majesty. We develop lighting systems which can go up and down with great artistry to give us a sense of being in an unreal world far from all the harsh glare of life. Believe me, our fathers were nearer to truth with their plain meetinghouses, their hard benches, and their willingness to listen to a man expound on what God expected from them.

Much of our religion has become so informal that it smacks of a political rally. I have heard prayers that disdain the use of the more formal King James "thou" and talk to God as if He were the man next door. All of this seems to me in the nature of the Rotarian custom of calling everybody by a nickname. It is like meeting the President of the United States for the first time and calling him Lyndon. Woe unto us when we lose our sense of the holiness of the Almighty and minimize the awesome and indeed terrifying experience of coming into His presence.

Let us make sure that we understand that God is not a celestial politician seeking our votes. He does not depend upon us and upon our approval. He does not exist to run our errands. He is not to be used by us at all, but we are to remember first, last, and always that we are His children only when we find His will and do it.

There is an old cathedral in the city of Cuzco, Peru. The Roman Catholic faith in this city has been influenced by some of the Indian paganism and around Christmas time they put up a neon sign on the church: "Olé Jesus." Translated, it reads "Hooray for Jesus!" I am sure that our Lord appreciates our enthusiastic response, but let us be very clear that he does not need our applause and I doubt if he really wants our cheers. Remember the verse in the Book of Job which speaks of God as one who brings "rain on a land where no man is" (38:26). Do you suppose Job is trying to tell us that God is bigger than our limited human concerns?

God is to be found and God is to be obeyed. He gave His laws to Moses in the Ten Commandments, and today we wonder if they are not unnecessarily severe and negative. We would prefer something more positive. But the Jew understood that God commands and man obeys. Through all these centuries it has been proved true that to accept the Commandments is to live and to deny them is to die. Nothing in our modern life has changed the reality of these judgments which are true and righteous altogether.

In the closing part of the Gospel of St. Mark there is a verse which at first sounds out of place. It occurs in the story of the appearances of the resurrected Christ to the disciples. "And he said to them, 'Go into all the world and preach the gospel to the whole creation. He who believes and is baptized will be saved; but he who does not believe will be condemned'" (16:15-16). Is this not unnecessarily harsh coming from the resurrected Christ? The King James Version has it that those who do not believe will be damned. This hard word needs to be spoken to this generation. He does not adjust himself to suit the desires of even his well-meaning followers, and the sooner we understand this truth, the better for us. Let us not forget that God made us in His image but that we did not make Him in our image. To try to move Him into a better position will only bring the disaster upon us which came to Uzzah when he tried to interfere with the Ark.

There came to my desk a paper from one of our theological seminaries. Included in it was a tribute to a retiring professor written by an alumnus. The tribute said that this man had presented "a reasonable Deity who was acceptable and understandable to scientist and saint." I said to myself that God must be very pleased that somebody made Him acceptable to some people. I shuddered that anyone would think that this is the task of a theologian. We need great poets, it is true, who can "justify the ways of God to men," as Milton once put it. But actually, what we need more than anything else is for men to declare what God's will is and to warn us that a refusal to do it is death. A president of the University of New Hampshire, traveling through the mountains of his state in October, was heard to murmur, "I hope I'll never get used to it." May we never get used to the greatness of the moral law, the glory of freedom, and the majesty of God. May we have grace enough to know that these are not to be maneuvered but accepted.

❦ 2 ❧

Always in Debt

I am under obligation both to Greeks and to barbarians, both to the wise and to the foolish: so I
am eager to preach the gospel to you also who are
in Rome.   ROMANS 1:14–15

ONE OF the bishop's privileges in The Methodist Church is to
welcome young men into the ministry. After a boy has been on trial
with us for three or four years, the time comes when he stands
before an annual conference and answers questions read by the
bishop. The questions have come down to us from John Wesley,
and they have been little changed throughout the years. One of
them is: "Are you in debt so as to embarrass you in your work?" I
never heard a young man answer "yes," and I do not know what I
would do if he did. I have found out later that some of them had
pretty heavy financial obligations, and I have come to the conclusion
that they are hard to embarrass. Maybe they should be asked if they
are in debt so as to embarrass anyone else.

Some time ago I was reading St. Paul's letter to the Romans and
these words captured my attention: "I am under obligation both to
Greeks and to barbarians, both to the wise and to the foolish."
Supposing, I thought, that St. Paul were seeking admission into one
of our Conferences and this question about debt were put to him.
He would answer, "Am I in debt so as to embarrass me? I sure am.
I owe everybody from the cultured to the crude; from the wise to

the foolish; from the good to the bad. Why," he might say, "if I lived a thousand years I could not pay back what I owe."

He was saying, of course, that a man is always in debt and that no one can ever say he owes no one. We are born owing so much that none of us ever gets clear of obligations. So far as debt is concerned, the affluent society is no different from the poorest society. This point of view presents us with a rather grim outlook. For the truth is, and this is the first thing I want to say,

We Fear Debt.

On this subject I speak with some authority. I cannot remember a time in my childhood when my family was clear of debt. Although it always seemed that we were just about to make it, we never did. My father would call a family conference and tell us why we could not do what we had set our hearts on. But, he would tell us, we only had so many more payments on this particular debt, and then we ought to have a little more money to give us more spending choices. It never worked out that way, and while it was pleasant to dream and plan, debts were a part of my youth. I hated them and I feared them.

When my wife and I were first married, we had a friend who was a retired manufacturer and very wealthy. He often said to me, "A young man should be willing to go into debt and have no fear of owing money." I believed him with my head but not with my heart, for the constant pressure of debts had been a continual worry all my childhood.

A few years ago in India a young missionary took us out through the country to visit some of the many small villages. He told us that these people were born into debt and they hardly ever escaped. Living always on the edge of starvation and want, the peasants had to borrow from time to time and always at outrageous interest rates. They spent their lives hoping to escape debt, but they never got free. So no matter what their legal status was, they actually lived in financial slavery until they died.

The sharecropper in this country went through the same experience. In hopes that a good year would get him even, he found always that he was not quite clear when the crop was harvested. There was nothing to do but go to the store where he could get credit to feed and clothe his family after a fashion, and sink deeper and deeper into debt every year. There comes to such people a deadening despair and hopelessness. They ask, "What is the use?" In a moment of realism such people know that things will never be better and that they will never be free. It is against this kind of dull, hopeless struggle that we wage our war on poverty. Such people are never in a position to make the contributions we have a right to expect from our citizens. They never know the joy of playing a real part in the nation's life.

A friend of mine who has directed a social agency for young men and boys for forty years in the Elephant and Castle district of London, once told me of his family's fear of sickness when he was a boy. Sickness meant loss of work and going into debt. They were urged to "work it off" when they felt ill. Those of us who are more fortunate must not forget the burden of debt on the poor. It is a very real thing around the world, and it is of concern to all of us.

We are also afraid of being in debt intellectually. We want to be known as men of new ideas and originality, and consequently we are tempted to claim as our own what came from another. There was an American preacher whose wife published some of his sermons after he died. An English preacher read them and thought they sounded strangely familiar. When he checked them carefully, he found they had been appropriated with little change from one of his own books. It was such a flagrant case that the publisher settled in a hurry, but this did not appease the Englishman's anger. Of course if the American had lived, he would never have consented to the publishing of his material. Still, the theft was a shameful thing. No preacher should use another's material in such a way as to feel embarrassed if that other man appeared unexpectedly in the congregation while he was using the material. If it is uncomfortable to be in debt, it is even worse to be in debt and not to confess it.

Almost any writer is tempted constantly to minimize his obligations to other writers. Most of our material comes from somebody else, but we ought to think it through, give it the style of our personalities so that it has the stamp of our minds. While few of us will ever be regarded as original thinkers, all of us have something of our own to contribute. The man who thinks he is expressing an original idea will most likely find that a Greek said it better five or six hundred years before the birth of Christ. To confess our debts does not make us poor but rich, and plagiarism is the sin of a small mind.

A country boy was given some money by his father and told to see the circus. He rode into the town, tied up his horse, and followed the crowd. In a little while the band came down the street, followed by the wild animals in cages, the acrobats, and the clowns. The boy watched it to the end and then rode home again. His father was surprised to see him so soon, and he was even more surprised that he still had his money. "Didn't you see the circus?" he asked. "Sure," the boy answered, "it came down the street and it was free." The fear of having to pay and the desire to save money keeps many a man watching a parade but never seeing the show. Our fear of debt makes us settle for too little.

The second thing to notice is the opposite side of the coin:

We Seek Independence and Freedom.

The goal of life becomes the attainment of self-sufficiency.

There is a sense in which this is the legitimate process of growing up. The boy wants to arrive at the place where he can be independent of his father and be his own boss. He imagines a time when no one can tell him to be in at midnight or to mow the lawn. The girl thinks it will be wonderful when her mother cannot tell her to use less make-up and to wear her skirts longer. There is a time in life when parents are taskmasters whose chief function is to prevent their children from doing what they want to do and to make them do what they do not want to do. Then it is that to be free to do as one pleases seems like heaven. We learn one day that a man's real troubles begin when he can do as he pleases.

There is the slavery to money. The young couple begin bravely with a budget. It all makes sense on paper, and it is a new adventure to plan just how much can be spent for each need. Of course, it never quite works out that way, and the budget becomes increasingly a burden and an irritation. Someday, says the wife, may we have enough money to spend without having to worry about the budget! Happiness is a situation where an extra hundred dollars is not a matter of life and death. Madison Avenue spends most of its time and skill in persuading us that financial success is the true goal of life.

The lure of travel is an appeal to freedom from local responsibilities and obligations. The dream of many a man is to be free to wander at will and see strange sights in faraway places. Some of us whose work makes it necessary to travel a good deal have lost this spirit. When we have a holiday, we want to stay home. But to be free from daily obligations and roam the world at will seems the ideal situation to most people.

The boy longs for the day when he can talk to his father man to man. No longer will he be the inexperienced youth expected to take advice and be told what he can do. The time will come, he hopes, when he will be a man, able to express his opinions on equal terms with his father. Maybe he will have children and can do unto them as his father has been doing unto him. Freedom from parental authority lurks in the minds of young people as a state very much to be desired.

The student who sits gratefully at the feet of a fine teacher wishes for a day when he knows enough about the subject to be treated as an equal. It is not that he does not respect the teacher and indeed he honors him and will be forever appreciative. But he is aiming at that time when the professor will ask his opinion and consult him as a colleague. A good many years ago I was invited to teach preaching at my old seminary. I shall not forget the high moment when a former professor addressed me in an assembly as "Professor Kennedy." I had arrived.

There is a sense in which independence is the Protestant promise in man's relation to God. We do not have to pray through the priest or by way of the saints. No professional or expert is necessary to represent us before God. Each man is a priest and every man is confronted by God directly. The hierarchy may be necessary for the housekeeping duties connected with the institution, but it is not necessary to get me introduced to God. We sometimes forget that this means terrifying responsibilities for the individual. But the ability of every Christian man to enter directly into fellowship with God is a precious heritage.

There was once a boy who found a dime in the road. He was so impressed with getting something for nothing that for the rest of his life, he walked with his eyes on the road. After forty years he had picked up nearly thirty-five thousand buttons, more than fifty thousand pins, about four dollars in loose change, a bent back, and a terrible disposition. This is the reward facing the man who makes a career out of being independent. Unless he is careful, he will miss the richest things in life.

Let us, therefore, look at a third proposition which will sound like bad news. It is simply that

We Can Never Be Out of Debt.

The whole dream is false and the goal is unattainable. From the day we are born until the day we die, we owe more than we can pay, no matter how long we live or how rich we get.

My parents died before I could do much to repay them what I owed. My father was not alive when The Methodist Church, in a weak moment, no doubt, elected me a bishop. If he had been present when that happened, he would have thought it a greater honor than to have a son President of the United States. My mother, who gave so much that I am just now beginning to realize it, never received any proper recognition of my debt to her. This troubles me many times, and if there were a way to make plain to my parents how much I owe them, it would be joy. One thing is perfectly clear, and that is that I could never come near being clear of my obligations to them. Let any man or woman think two minutes of the love and sacrifice invested in them, and they will not talk any more about being self-sufficient.

I remember my teachers, especially a young man who taught my Sunday School class when I was about eight years old. We were an ornery bunch, and if anybody has trouble believing the theological doctrine of original sin, let him teach a class of eight-year-old boys. Yet that young fellow was patient and faithful, and now and again took us to the river on a Saturday. I have thought since how many things he must have preferred doing on those occasions and how often he must have been tempted to push us in. I wish there were some way to tell him what he has meant to me through the years and how many things he said I still remember. And when I think of all the other fine teachers who have enriched my life with their example and wisdom, the debt is so staggering that I am in despair.

Consider your neighbors. We do not seem to find time to be very neighborly with the people who live near us. But their good will is shown in a hundred little ways, and it lifts up my heart to know they are there. If I needed help, they would respond, and if anything happened to me, my wife would find them ready to help her. We live in a big city, but there is genuine friendship and concern all about us which we are aware of when we stop to think about it for a moment. Every once in a while a stranger does something for me so unexpected and so wonderful that a man wants to shout.

During the 1964 presidential election, there appeared on a few bumpers: "Please, Uncle Sam. I would rather do it myself." The first time I saw it I was speechless. Did the fellow know what he was saying? Did he ever count up the things he received from society and the extent to which he was dependent on his brethren for his life? Consider those who came before us and built the cities, the transportation systems, the schools. I would like to have such a man build these things himself for twenty-four hours and see how he comes out. His sentiment is nonsense, and only thoughtless people ever believe that they do not need the help of government in maintaining themselves.

The man who began with nothing and achieved success is tempted to speak of himself as a self-made man. All this does is relieve the Almighty from a mighty embarrassing responsibility. No man is able to claim that he is a self-made man. Every one of us had friends who strengthened us by believing in us and giving us encouragement. Let us not minimize our own efforts with false humility, but let us not forget how much we owe to other people. When a football player makes a long run, there was a key block which sprung him loose. There are always key blocks when we break away for a big gain, and only small men will forget it.

Many years ago a wealthy student at Williams College was accused of defacing college property and was sent to see President Mark Hopkins. He came in arrogantly, took out his purse, and asked how much were the damages. This was too much for President Hopkins, who commanded the young man to sit down. "No man," said the president, "can pay for what he receives here. Can you pay for the sacrifice of Colonel Williams who founded the college? Can you pay for the half-paid professors who have remained here to teach when they could have gone elsewhere? Every student here is a charity case." So are we all.

The last thing to say is that

Acknowledging Our Debts Brings Us a Strange Joy.

This process is paradoxical. We learn as we grow older how often a seeming contradiction leads us to a higher logic. We follow a hard path and come to a magnificent view which reveals the meaning of the journey. Strange it is that giving up means receiving, and that humility is victory.

You see, the acceptance of our status as debtors destroys our pride, and that is good. It brings us to the end of a vain search, and finally we accept the truth that we are loved. We are filled with such thankfulness that our hearts overflow with joy. It is the discovery that all our giving is merely a drop in the bucket when it comes to settling our accounts. While it is true that giving is more blessed than receiving, being the object of loving concern brings a blessedness all its own.

The Good Samaritan is a case in point. But do you suppose he might have been a man who realized how often he had received? Could he possibly have fallen among thieves himself at one time and found unexpected help from a stranger? Was he a man aware of how much other people had done for him? Nobody can know about these matters, but it is interesting to speculate, for men with no sense of owing are less likely to be generous or helpful in a crisis. May the good Lord save us from the hard hearts which are formed in those who consider themselves beyond obligation.

One of the amazing things is that people who do the most seem to be least aware of it. There is never the slightest tendency to let others do the difficult work or to regard themselves as excused from the hard jobs. Those whose lives have been models of service never seem to realize they have been making sacrifices. Rather, at the root of their characters is a sense of something owing which is sheer joy to acknowledge.

God has brought us the spirit of joyous obligation through Christ. The Gospel is glad announcement that God loves the world and gave His son for it. We are the ones for whom Christ died. We discover that before we sought him, he sought us. Christianity is a proclamation that we are always in debt and service to our brethren is our privilege. All of the great Church Festivals have this as their basic theme. For our debt is not one that makes us unhappy and worried, but one that sets us free from arrogance.

When Abraham Lincoln was killed, his body was taken to Springfield by way of the large cities in the East. Usually the funeral procession went from the railroad station to the city hall, where the body would lay in state and the people would come to express their sorrow and respect. As the hearse was moving slowly through the streets of New York City which were lined with thousands of people, a big, husky woodsman pressed forward through the crowd to see it. He jostled a few people and stepped on the feet of a man who cried out angrily, "Don't walk on my feet!" The big fellow was instantly apologetic and said, "Excuse me, sir, but I must see the coffin." "Why must you?" asked the man. "Two of my brothers died in the same cause he did," replied the woodsman sadly. "Besides," he said proudly, "he was one of my craft and I could never go back to the woods without seeing and blessing his coffin." The crowd parted and let him through.

That man was expressing what is in the heart of all men when they see life clearly. We are forever in debt and we must express our thanks. All that we have is little enough to give, and so the Christian finds joy in his giving. For no matter how long we live or how much we are able to give, it is never enough. Let us remember that and rejoice in it. For to be aware that we are debtors is one of Christ's gifts to his disciples.

✥ 3 ✥

Fresh Every Morning

And Moses said to them, "Let no man leave any
of it till the morning." But they did not listen to
Moses; some left part of it till the morning, and it
bred worms and became foul; and Moses was
angry with them.   EXODUS 16:19–20

WE BEGIN with an old story from the Book of Exodus. The Israelites
wandering in the wilderness complained a good deal about many
things. They murmured against Moses because they remembered
food in Egypt and they were experiencing short rations in the desert.
Then God promised them meat in the evening and bread in the
morning, and quails came at the close of the day, for their meat and
manna fell on the ground in the morning. A desert plant called the
tamarisk exudes a white sweet substance that has food value, and
when it falls to the ground it crystallizes. The Bible says it looks like
frost. They gathered it and prepared it, but they were warned by
Moses not to gather more than enough for a man and his family for
one day. As is always the case, there were those who thought they
knew more than God, and they collected enough for several days.
They wanted security. But the next morning they found their
manna had a foul odor and was full of worms.

This is not a word encouraging carelessness and improvidence.
Jesus said about the same thing in the Lord's Prayer when he taught
us the phrase, "Give us this day our daily bread," which is to say,
bread for the day. We are being told that there are some things we
cannot save up for the future, and there are some values which can

be neither pickled nor embalmed. There in the wilderness, God was teaching the people that the great values of life have to be gathered fresh every morning. Let us think of this and some of its implications.

We may as well begin with the obvious fact that

Men Seek Protection Against the Future.

There is nothing new in this, and society has always been expected to help men in their defense against unforeseen accidents and dangers. But in our time, security has become a subject of great debate, so that if you want to start an argument, all you need do is mention "the welfare state" or talk about "creeping socialism." We are concerned today about the growing power of government, and we try to determine how far it ought to be allowed to go and where the limit should be drawn.

Some of the debate is unrealistic and probably hypocritical. It would be much more convincing, for example, if the man who is arguing against social security were a poor man who had nothing to protect him in his old age. But the men who usually argue the loudest are those who have reserves laid up and for whom retirement will be no financial problem. The farmer who is supposed to be the last rugged individualist in our society seldom refuses the government subsidy which holds the price up and keeps him prosperous. The man who may talk eloquently against government contributions to institutions is often the first man to ask what government funds are available when he is elected to the board of trustees of a church college or hospital.

Still, the debate ought to go on because this is a serious subject and we must be aware of its implications. It is quite clear, however, that we are not going back to some fancied period of free enterprise when there was no government support of any social institution.

In our personal lives we have this same longing for protection and security. It is hard for us to realize now that when insurance was first introduced, a good many religious people argued that it was unchristian not to trust God. We have not heard that argument in a long time. A friend of mine confessed not long ago that he was insurance-poor. He said he was spending so much money on all kinds of insurance that the family never had the money to do what they would like to do now. But, he added, they were fairly sure they were protected against the possible disasters of tomorrow. This seems to be a poor kind of arrangement.

Retirement is certainly more in our minds today than it was a concern in the past. For one thing, we have a chance to live longer and we are being forced to quit our jobs earlier. Retirement is never much of a problem if the chances are that you are going to die before you reach that age anyway. But when it looks likely that most of us will live a number of years after our company tells us we can no longer work, it becomes a vital problem and we get concerned about old-age protection.

This influences young people's attitude toward their jobs. The day when any young man on the basis of nerve and a few dollars could start his own business seems to be fading. When we go to work for a corporation, we want to know about such things as sick leave, vacation allowance, and retirement policy. The circumstances of our modern life have forced us to be more interested in these matters, and perhaps if we are not careful, we will become overconcerned about them.

There is an old legend that when the Israelites were being pursued by the Egyptians and they came to the Red Sea, nothing happened until the first man waded in. Whatever else we may think about security, and may the debate continue, we ought never to have a society where a man is afraid to be the first one to wade in if the cause is important enough and good enough.

The second thing we ought to note is that however we may feel about this question of safety and welfare, we must realize that

Physical Security Does Not Settle the Main Problems.

Jesus put it with his usual insight and succinctness when he said, "Man does not live by bread alone." Christianity is a materialistic religion, and it never counsels us to retreat from life and live in some artificial, safe environment. But it is always careful to point out that after we have solved the physical problems, we still have not dealt with the main issues of being men.

While attending the Central Methodist Conference of Scandinavia, I met a young doctor and his family from Denmark. I asked him one day if it were true that Denmark has the highest suicide rate in the world. He said it was true. When I asked him why, he said he did not know the reason. Usually, he added, if people get angry or upset, they may shoot somebody, but in Denmark they shoot themselves. Yet Denmark has a socialized society that cares for people fairly adequately. One would think that if security is the problem, then this clean little country would be a solution to it.

In Russia one is not aware of cities full of happy, smiling people. There is usually a certain drabness that communism seems to produce, and the elimination of uncertainty regarding work and income does not result in a utopia of human content. Indeed, Russians seem to be wanting more variety and more individual difference. They are asking for unequal salaries, since some jobs are obviously worth more than others to the state. They want to own things for themselves as they discover that private property is one of the foundations of human dignity. They would like to invest money and receive interest on it, and this is being allowed. If I were a Russian Communist I would fear "creeping capitalism." The welfare state of England has solved some problems, but certainly you could hardly prove that Englishmen in general are happier than other people. New Zealand is a managed economy, but I saw no indication that New Zealanders are more at ease with their environment and less worried than other people.

Let America be aware of progress in social responsibility and rejoice. But no one will suggest seriously that we have solved the main issues of humanity and are now a contented, satisfied people. I remember that in 1951 at the World Methodist Conference in Oxford, the late Dr. W. E. Sangster preached one night. He spoke some words directly to Americans which some of my colleagues resented. He said that Americans are a wonderful people with better homes, more automobiles, and greater wealth than any nation has ever known. But, he added, "I notice that you also write more books on 'how to be happy.'" The physical side of life is important as the Gospel recognizes. It is not, however, the complete story, and the solving of our physical problems does not bring us contentment as we were promised.

Neither is the economic side of things the whole story. As a young man I heard this theory promulgated so often that I began to believe it. There were discussions about the economic interpretation of the Constitution of the United States. There were Marxist intepretations of history that preached dollars and cents as the final issue. America, according to this point of view, was born not out of a revolution for freedom, but out of an attempt on the part of the landed classes to improve their economic condition. And all of this is at best a half-truth and our time indicates its falseness. We must never say that the improvement of the physical conditions of life is unimportant, and we are committed to a minimum comfort and security for all our people. Other things being equal, it is better to be rich than to be poor Quite so! But we must not assume that man will find salvation on this route.

I picked up a statistic some time ago which impressed me very much. In the first period, what was the biggest selling product at the New York World's Fair? Aspirin! In the first six months, there was sold over a half million aspirin tablets—with more than ten thousand orange-flavored for the children. Apparently the brave new world is full of headaches, and thinking about all the physical progress of tomorrow does not create peace of mind.

A third thing to note is that

The Important Things Cannot Be Gathered in Advance.

This is what the old story is saying to us and this is a lesson which the Bible would teach us.

Take patriotism, for example. Why did Samuel Johnson in his famous *Dictionary* written in the eighteenth century define patriotism as "the last refuge of a scoundrel"? It must have been because there were men then as there are now who make patriotism a racket. It can become a narrow, bitter attack on all who disagree or refuse to conform. It is easy to mouth slogans which had some meaning in 1776 but in 1966 are high-sounding, windy abstractions. Such patriots have gathered eloquent sentiments and tried to embalm them. Patriotism, of course, is being grateful for our heritage now and seeking to serve the country at this particular moment. Once we try to keep yesterday's sentiment for the future, it begins to smell. The man making a profit out of his patriotism is something which decent people despise. Time does make ancient good uncouth as James Russell Lowell said, and patriotism which divides and creates distrust and suspicion is like the manna which some of the Israelites tried to gather for the future. It breeds worms.

We do not consider enough how tenuous is the achievement of civilization and culture. We do not realize how easy it is for the people to lose what many generations have gained. The eminent historian Arnold Toynbee has made clear that the most dangerous period for a civilization is when it thinks it is safe and no longer needs to face further challenges. There is a sense in which civilization has to be gathered fresh every morning or it will be lost. Toynbee told about a lost city overgrown and buried by the jungle. Somebody found it, and after cutting away the bushes and vines, and digging out the roots, there were the remains of a once splendid city. The historian went on to say that the jungle waits like a beast to spring upon a careless civilization. Just so soon as people no longer consider their life worthy of their sacrifice, their end is in sight.

But we have had an example in our own time. Not too long ago one was not well educated unless he had been to Germany and taken a Ph.D. in a German university. This was true not only of science but of theology. Overnight, historically speaking, Germany lost its supremacy and went back to a savagery unequaled in all history. It is still a shock to realize what happened in that unhappy country, and I have visited former concentration camps and seen pictures of atrocities that made me sick. But let no one say it cannot happen here.

The Church is always on the edge of the abyss. Somebody once said to a churchman that Christianity was on its last legs, and he replied that it is always on its last legs. Just so soon as enough people decide that the free church is no longer worth preserving, we are finished. We do not offer any economic or social advantage to people. The Church has to win its life every morning, or it will lose it. There is precious little comfort in the thought that nineteen hundred years of Christianity is only one generation away from annihilation.

Consider education. Young people sometimes assume that if they go to college and get an A.B. degree, they are educated. But there is nothing more disillusioning than to see the average college graduate ten years after he has left college. He often has become opinionated, prejudiced, and narrow. New ideas one time challenged and excited him, but now they frighten him. A book is now something his wife dusts. His reading is confined to the sports page of the daily newspaper. Education is gathered fresh every morning or it spoils.

This is especially true of marriage, and whenever a man and a woman decide that the wedding was an ending and not a beginning, they are on the way to trouble. For a marriage cannot be preserved against the future; it has to be won fresh each day. Marriage is the beginning of one of life's greatest experiences. It is the beginning of an adventure which grows more wonderful with the years. It is not the end of anything.

Think of this strange thing we call character which is a network of attitudes and habits we build as a defense against time. Character is a complete denial of the theological heresy that once in Grace, we are always in Grace. I can recall yet the shock that came to me when a man I thought I knew very well and trusted completely was indicted for stealing money from his company. I would have trusted him with my last cent. But one day his character was weighed and found wanting. Character is on trial every day and character is never complete.

A young man once fell in love with a girl and saw the starlight in her eyes when he proposed. I saw that once long ago myself and many of you did. He bought a ring to give her, but he was poor and it wasn't a very big diamond. He said to her apologetically, "It is not a very big stone." But she replied, "It is as big as we make it." Ah, that is it! The important things in life can be made bigger with every passing year, if we remember that they have to be gathered fresh each day.

Now the last thing to say is that

God Provides for Us Daily.

Israel's history taught us this lesson. The Jews have never been safe or secure, except for rather brief moments in their history. Oftentimes it was almost literally true that Israel went to bed at night not knowing if in the morning she would still be a free nation. The kings were judged not by their immediate successes, but by whether or not they trusted God and preserved the loyalty of the people to Him. But the Jews have given the world two great religions, and they have taught us one of the most necessary lessons, namely, that while we must face each new year in danger, we can also face it in faith.

Jesus taught his disciples to regard evil as sufficient unto the day, and he urged them to take no thought of the morrow. This was not an encouragement to improvidence but a reminder to recognize the impossibility of providing security for ourselves. We are dependent upon God's care by day, and we claim it every morning with confidence. We never drift beyond His love and care.

Dietrich Bonhoeffer was a German Christian imprisoned by the Nazis and finally executed before the Allied armies could set him free. His writings from the concentration camp have given fresh insight into deep meanings of the Christian faith. In one of his letters he wrote, "I believe God will give us all the power we need to resist in all the time of distress. But he never gives it in advance lest we should rely upon ourselves and not on him alone." Ah yes, He does not give it to us in advance and we have to receive it fresh every morning. This life we live in Christ is one of the most wonderful experiences men can know. We cannot be safe but we can be saved. We cannot be secure but we can be unafraid. We cannot live cautiously but we can live adventurously.

A sociologist interviewed some teenagers regarding their impressions of their homes and parents. Strangely enough, he discovered that those who had been brought up permissively were not very appreciative of that experience, and those who had been disciplined were grateful for it. One girl told the interviewer that she lived in an apartment in a big city, and after supper in the summer the children on the block gathered in the streets to play. But after a while one would say that she had to go home because her mother had told her to be in before eight o'clock. Or a father would whistle and a boy would have to leave. A mother would call and others would have to go. The girl said, "They would all go. It would get dark and I would be there alone, waiting for my father or my mother to call me in. They never did."

And I thought to myself, God is not like that. He has established the moral law which means we must reap what we have sown. He puts high demands upon us and seems more interested in making us great than in making us happy. But there comes a time when we know that this strictness and concern is not because He hates us but because He loves us. The discovery of God's love for us is the greatest experience we will ever have. It means we can trust Him to care for us and give us what we need every day. In this faith we live our lives in confidence, gathering what we must have to live by fresh every morning.

4

Dwelling Place of Wonder

Thou whose glory above the heavens is chanted
   by the mouth of babes and infants,
thou hast founded a bulwark because of thy foes,
   to still the enemy and the avenger.

PSALM 8:1-2

THE MOOD of true religion is one of wonder and awe. Whenever religious people have lost this mood, you may be sure they have lost their way. Standing before the majesty of God and seeing all the wonder of His involvement in human life, man breaks into poetry if he is able, but at the very least he stands in silence. Perhaps nothing indicates more clearly that our religion has become profitless and stale than the rarity of this experience of awe.

It may seem strange to this generation if we suggest that the church is the preserver of this experience. But in a day when few people seem to have a good word for the church and the clamor for its renewal or its elimination is loud in the land, allow me the privilege of calling to your attention its glory and its greatness.

A few years ago the eminent drama critic, John Mason Brown, in an article in the *Saturday Review* referred to Robert Emmet Sherwood's definition of the theater as "the dwelling place of wonder." Many of us will know what he meant, if we have experienced the theater at its best. We will remember occasions when a great drama lifted us high and opened the gates of heaven. It was a time of inspiration and vision. It seemed to us that for an hour or so we saw the truth about men and life.

But I want to suggest that the church deserves that definition much more than the theater. It is not always true, of course, but here is a description of its essential nature. Halford Luccock, of blessed memory, one time referred to a church as "a society for the prevention of astonishment." Those of us who participate in its worship regularly know how often it has been guilty of this description. A church can become deadly, dull, boring, and stuffy. But think with me for a little while concerning the church as the dwelling place of wonder.

To begin with, we should observe

The Wonder of Its History.

History can be a dull affair, but when it reveals to us a small thing becoming great or a weak thing becoming strong or a powerful idea entering into the hearts of men and transforming their existence, it becomes drama. You will recall that St. Paul said Christ had made his life a glorious pageant.

The Christian church began at Pentecost, which was a Greek term for the Jewish Feast of Weeks. It was a harvest festival, and it commemorated in particular the giving of the Law. But for the Christian church it is the time when the Holy Spirit came upon the disciples who were gathered together in one place in Jerusalem. The story is in the second chapter of Acts, and it relates that the first Christians were given the power to speak in different languages so that each man heard the good news in his own tongue. Most of the people who were gathered there, however, thought these men were drunk, which is not a very propitious beginning for any new movement. But out of that beginning came the Christian church, although nobody at the time would have thought it would go very far or amount to very much. Such emotional experiences are not uncommon and hardly ever does much come from them.

Yet from this beginning, the church began to expand and grow. It was severely persecuted and more than once it has seemed to be on its last legs. Those ancient days have been reborn in our time, and we saw Nazi Germany attempt to stamp out the Christian church by changing it into an arm of the Nazi state. In Russia we have watched a society concentrate its full power against the church and preach to the people that it is nothing but superstition and myth. Oddly enough, those who would make the church weak and useless seem curiously silent about its heroism and sacrifice under the attack of fascists and communists. Little attention is paid to Albert Einstein's testimony that when the editors of great papers and the professors of universities surrendered, it was the church that proved to be the stumbling block over which Hitler fell.

That it should have existed at all is a mystery and a wonder. That it should have spread triumphantly around the world and challenged emperors is a miracle. Somebody is always prophesying its coming demise, but as someone pointed out, before you can have a funeral, you must have a willing corpse. Its history seems to bear testimony to something eternal within it and a phoenix power to rise out of ashes.

To list its accomplishments is to recount the great achievements of our Western civilization. After the destruction of Rome it became the preserver of learning. In the monasteries the dim light of culture was kept from going out. The great universities came from the church, and even as late as America's beginnings, the early institutions of higher learning were church sponsored. If anyone doubts the Christian church's contribution to education, let him consider the small colleges which were established throughout the Middle West and the West by Christian people who wanted their children and their ministers to have the privileges of learning.

Like any institution, it has known evil days and corruption. Turn back to the Reformation which began in the fourteenth century and reached its climax in Martin Luther's witness in the sixteenth century. The unity of the church was broken but the corrupt practices were eliminated and the freedom of Christian men was preserved. Or look to the eighteenth century in England when the evangelical revival flowed out across the land and men like John

Wesley brought new life to a very sick institution. It has been a constant preacher of righteousness and a continuing opponent of tyranny.

Today it needs to be renewed as it always does. But let no man think that renewal should mean destruction or that two thousand years of history are meaningless. When I was in Australia a few years ago, some of the brethren were asking whether America was going fascist. They had been reading of the strange and weird tactics of the far-right extremists. I said to them that America would not go fascist any more than it would go communist because of the Christian church. Dedicated to the dignity of the individual and to God's demand for freedom for every man, it will be the destruction of autocratic control of ideas and opinion from the right or the left.

A boy brought a report card home that was quite satisfactory. His father asked if he were first in his class and he said no, a girl was first and he was second. Said his father, "Did you let a mere girl beat you?" The boy answered, "Well, girls are not so mere today as they used to be." And the church which to so many people seems merely an institution, proves to be one of man's greatest stories when its history is told.

In the second place, let us consider that the church deals with

The Wonder of Life.

Life began so long ago and has persisted through all sorts of dangers. It has been under the care of an unseen and Almighty Power, which the church does not let us forget.

Some wonders of nature are talked about so much that to see them is anticlimax. But one place where that can never happen is the Grand Canyon of the Colorado. J. B. Priestley once remarked that if anybody was disappointed in the Grand Canyon, he would be disappointed at the Day of Judgment. There, dug deep by the Colorado River, is a record of the long past. As a man said when he looked at it for the first time, "Something happened there." Indeed it did. And something began millions of years ago and has been happening ever since.

We look upon the living things of the desert, and from somebody who knows the story, it is exciting drama. I heard a man talk one time about a cactus which swells up and stores water during the relatively brief rainy season and lets it down to the roots gradually for the rest of the year. It keeps itself alive by a miracle. There was a naturalist who spent his life studying one species of spider. When asked why he could give so much time to this one small creature, his only answer was because it was very interesting, that's why.

Now we are being told that there may be life on other planets and that someday we may exchange visits. The cynic wants to know what this will do to our religion. Well, all it will do to my religion is to make me want to say in the words of the hymn, "How great Thou art." In the drabness of daily existence we can forget the miracle of life and the drama of its growth and preservation.

The main issue between communism and democracy is not economics or even political theory. In recent years these two systems come closer together so far as economics is concerned. The communists are demanding more freedom and the free-enterprise societies are exhibiting a greater sense of social responsibility. The socialism of New Zealand is certainly something very different from the tyrants' control of Russia or China. The main difference is the definition of man. Communism assumes that a single man isn't important except as he serves the state and he can be sacrificed for some future good. But societies touched by the Christian faith can never look upon a single man as expendable. They are aware of the wonder of life.

The modern danger is a growing willingness to regard life as cheap. A military leader in all seriousness argued that in case of an atomic holocaust, only a certain percentage would be killed and a certain percentage would survive. When we begin to think of human beings in percentages, we are very, very sick. Yet already automation tends to regard persons as mere caretakers of the calculating machines and of less importance than the machines themselves.

We see brutality explode not only in actual war but in our cities during peace time. Gangs haunt the streets, seeking to destroy and hurt with no discernible reason back of their violence. We cold-bloodedly calculate the traffic casualities over a three-day weekend. If there was ever a time when we need an institution to keep us aware of the wonder of life, that time is now. The Christian church through the years gradually tamed the savages and made men aware of the preciousness of the gift of life. The church is always on the side of life, and it breaks through the glib talk to make us aware when people are at stake and human life is being desecrated.

Justice Douglas spoke some time ago about a meeting of federal field men to discuss the protests of citizens against plans for the spraying of sage brush in Wyoming. There was an old lady who opposed the plan because she said that the wild flowers would be destroyed. They thought it was hilariously funny, but Justice Douglas wrote, "Yet, was not her right to search out a banded cup or a tiger lily as inalienable as the right of stockmen to search out grass or the lumberman to claim a tree?" When commercialism takes over and living things are sacrificed for profit, look out! Thank God for the church which keeps us aware of the wonder of all life.

A third thing I want to speak of is the church's teaching about

The Wonder of Man.

It is hard for a generation that has been through two world wars to keep a sense of wonder about man himself. What a long trail we have followed and what a story is the growth of man! We may lose the sense of the 8th Psalm's insight:

> What is man that thou art mindful of him,
>   and the son of man that thou dost care for him?
> Yet thou hast made him little less than God,
>   and dost crown him with glory and honor.

4-5

When we look at man we have to begin with an awareness of his misery. A good many years ago when I was in theological seminary I wrote two or three theses on sin and, as one of my friends commented, at least I was writing on something I knew something about. One of the few Greek words I recall is *hamartia*. It is the term for sin and it means literally "to miss the mark." As in so many instances, the Greeks had a word for it. Missing the mark brings man to misery and despair.

Man is free, and when all the arguments about predestination and free will are over, we know we have made choices by looking into our own hearts. That the great God should give us this freedom is wonder enough, for one would suppose that He prefers unquestioning obedience. But no, He wanted someone with whom He could have fellowship and this meant that man must choose. This door opens into all kinds of possibilities for evil and betrayal. The mystery of suffering is always beyond our comprehension and exploration, but the main clue, in my mind, is in the freedom with which God has endowed man. Here is the beginning of his trouble and the source of his failure. It is also the guarantee of his greatness.

I was thinking some time ago that man no longer needs to fear any other creature. The wild beasts that threatened his life are now in a zoo to look at but not to run from. More and more the terrifying forces of nature are brought under control so that his ships can sail through the storms and his buildings will protect him from the elements. But just as one wants to rejoice in this conquest, he realizes that man is now his own chief enemy. We are not afraid of anything but ourselves. The danger that raises our fear is our own destructive powers and our own untamed lust for killing.

Yet the other side of that picture is the vision of the Psalmist which the church holds before us. Chesterton one time pointed out that you could not say to a crocodile eating his tenth missionary, "Stop, be a crocodile." But you can say to a man who is taking his tenth whiskey, "Stop, be a man." There is the image of the Almighty upon us and the stamp of the King. Out of the misery of man there rises the greatness of man.

Think of the music men have written. I stand in awe before it because I do not understand it, and I marvel that anybody can think music and create it. Consider the great literature and the books which have ennobled our life.

Just when we want to think badly of all humanity, we see men sacrifice for a principle or argue and debate ideas. We see heroism, kindness, and love. Most of all we see Jesus Christ, and the wonder of this creature so full of misery and sin and so capable of greatness and love overwhelms us. We need something to keep us aware of man's misery and glory.

The greatness of the church is that it is neither sentimental nor is it hopelessly pessimistic. Its doctrine of humanity springs from the Bible, and it is the proclaimer of the wonderful news that out of the worst there comes the best. It has a message of something beyond our tragedy. It tells us of triumph which is realized out of suffering and defeat. Let no man oversimplify our nature or minimize the mystery of man's history and destiny. We are in need constantly of something to help us know the worst and believe in the best. That, my brethren, is the church.

Will Rogers one time commented cynically, "Most women leaving beauty parlors look as if they hadn't been waited on." All our attempts to pretty ourselves up and make us appear in a better light are in vain. None of this works, but the church looks at men "warts and all" and then points to beauty and hope. The church is the dwelling place of the wonder of man.

The last thing to say is that the church is the dwelling place of

The Wonder of God.

We shall find Him in many places as the Bible makes clear, but in a special way we shall discover Him in the sanctuary.

There has been a tendency in our time to minimize the transcendence of God. We have moved in the direction of socializing. It makes me cringe to hear advertising men, businessmen, and gogetting preachers try to make God one of them and not above them. The orthodox Jew often went to the other extreme. He would not even use the Name because it was holy. In the center of his temple there was the holy of holies which symbolized the awful presence of the Deity, and no one entered there but the High Priest. He was "the holy other," and at times they probably carried it too far. But they were nearer right than we are. God never became for the Jew an errand boy or a pal.

There has been a theological revolt and a return to a more Calvinistic approach to God. This too can go too far, but the impulse is healthy. We have been in need of a new awareness of the majesty and sovereignty of the great God. The easygoing pantheism which assumes that He is to be found everywhere in nature and thus is only an amorphous, impersonal tendency, is an insult to His Divine Majesty and destruction for us. We need to recover a sense of awe and of fear and trembling in His presence.

The church calls us to worship God and gives us the opportunity of coming together and entering His presence. It is the church which reminds us through its service of worship that His ways are not ours and that we are children of dust. It is the church that brings to us the vision of Isaiah who saw Him as high and lifted up.

Yet this is not the whole story by any means. If we believe in His transcendence, we also believe in His immanence. We believe in God who brings forgiveness to us and who removes our sin as far as the east is from the west. The transcendent God offers us fellowship and forgiveness which is an experience to shatter our complacency. Here we learn about His mercy as we sing the hymn,

> There's a wideness in God's mercy,
> Like the wideness of the sea;
> There is kindness in his justice,
> Which is more than liberty.

Here in the Christian church we come to a new understanding of the Incarnation. The opposites of transcendence and immanence meet together in the man Christ Jesus. When a man finds Christ, he knows that he has been blessed and saved through the ministry of the imperfect institution which we call the Christian church.

Some time ago a friend of mine who is not a churchman experienced a great tragedy. His only son, a brilliant boy headed for a medical career, was killed at a railroad crossing on his way back to the university. Everything went out of that man's life that made it worth living and he found it difficult to carry on his work. Whenever I met him and tried to talk with him, I found it impossible to find the word that could bring healing.

Some time after that event another friend of mine who was a very active churchman had a similar experience. His daugher was killed in an automobile accident. While the sorrow was deep, it did not overthrow his life. She was a Christian girl, and he spoke confidently of meeting her again. He published a little booklet giving excerpts from her letters and expressions of her faith. And I said to myself that here was a testimony to the wonder of the church. The loss for one man was final, but for the other man, it was sadness with eternal hope shining through it. I never realized before what it means to dwell within this fellowship of Christ and to know the power of its witness. Let no man take it lightly or speak ill of it. The Christian church is the dwelling place of wonder.

5

If You Go with Us

And if you go with us, whatever good the Lord
will do us, the same will we do to you.
NUMBERS 10:32

THE HEBREWS were encamped at Mount Sinai where they had
received the Commandments and other directions for organizing
their life. Now it was time for them to set out on their long journey
through the wilderness, and they needed a guide. Moses spoke to his
father-in-law, Hobab, about going with him. He told him that if he
would join the company, "We will do you good." But Hobab was
not moved by this appeal, and he said that he would not go with
them because he wanted to go home. Then Moses tried another
approach. He asked Hobab to go with him because he was needed
and he could do something for Israel. Said Moses, "Do not leave us,
I pray you, for you know how we are to encamp in the wilderness,
and you will serve as eyes for us." And then he came to the real
clincher, "And if you go with us, whatever good the Lord will do to
us, the same will we do to you."

Out of that ancient story we come to a curious conclusion. Hobab
was not moved by a selfish word that promised an advantage for
him. He only began to listen when the request was turned around
and he was asked to go with them because he was needed and he
could do something for Israel. But the final word was an invitation

to join a common cause and share God's blessings with one another. It is a great word for the present.

Moses began by saying

I Will Do Something for You.

This sounds like the best way to many people, and indeed we are told quite often that men are fundamentally selfish. If we are to persuade others to do something we want them to do, we will have to make them believe it is to their advantage. Moses began on this level.

What is the nature of man finally? Is it true that he is only a selfish animal and never makes any decision unless he can see a personal profit? It is argued often that even when human beings seem to be unselfish, they are actually acting only for their own advantage. It has become a rather popular assumption in our time that an unselfish appeal belongs in the same category with fairy stories and Sunday School teaching. Which is to say that realism demands that we come face to face with the futility of all idealism. Man, we are told, will do only what seems to him to be to his own advantage.

This is the interpretation of those who believe that society is made up of conflicting classes and that the class struggle is inevitable. It is the communist doctrine which declares that it is naïve to expect cooperation between capital and labor, between the poor and the rich, between those who have and those who have not. One class must rule, according to this theory, and the dictatorship of the proletariat must be established before justice is possible. The dream of classes functioning together cooperatively is impossible, according to this view, and workers are called upon to revolt, eliminate the owners, and establish their own rule.

This is in the background of the minds of those who attack the United Nations as a useless organization and who urge America to get out of it. Every nation, they assume, has only one selfish aim, and America had better go it alone with strength enough to enforce its will. Usually it is not put quite so baldly, but this is the belief of men who think that international cooperation can never be. No nation will cooperate with any other nation, they say, unless it can be sure that it is nationally advantageous to do so.

This is the spirit which rules most of our commercialism and especially our advertising. When we turn to that lowest and most vulgar of all public appeals—TV commercials—we discover this teaching in all its unlovely aspects. Whether we are worse off in my part of the country than in others, I do not know, but it is both amusing and disillusioning to listen to the TV hucksters selling cars. They always have the same two or three reasons for the special bargain. They are overstocked or they are trying to break a record. Always for some reason or other, profit is a secondary motive. The impression is given that if you will simply call the number or better still, visit the agency, they will practically pay you a bonus for just driving one of their cars off the lot. The trouble is that the listeners get hardened to this nonsense and after a little while they simply do not believe it.

There has grown up in our time a new group of religions which use Christian terminology but actually have little to do with the real gospel. They are faiths that claim to have some new psychological, modern, scientific approach, but essentially they are religions which promise to do something for people and make no demand that people shall do something for God. A man I knew years ago went into one of these new movements and became a minister of the new faith. He runs an advertisement in the paper nearly every Saturday which always begins with the words, "Let's talk about you." Not talk about God or Christ, mind you. The assumption is that here is a religion that will do something for you. It is all profit and no cost.

There is a modern tendency to turn our Christianity into a self-help religion. This has been an American emphasis, and the "peace of mind" brethren have appealed mainly to those who want Christianity to do something for them. Preaching has become a selling device to convince customers and clients that being a Christian is a very profitable matter. No one can deny that Christianity brings great joy to people, but when you divorce it from the Cross, you turn it into something it was never meant to be. It is no longer Christianity.

When the British Board of Trade prepared a "cost of living" index in 1900, they did not include anything in their normal working-class budget for butter or electricity. It was assumed that these were not items the working man ought to desire. But in 1962 when they made a similar study, they put into the budgets allowances for washing machines and TV sets. All of us are now of the opinion that these are necessities, and even if we cannot buy them for ourselves, we assume that society must furnish them. But you would be hard put to show that this new spirit has made us any happier or more at peace with ourselves. It is proper that we do more for each other, but it does not follow that the man who receives more of the benefits becomes automatically happier and more content.

In the second place, Moses made his appeal on the basis which seems to say that

You Can Do Something for Us.

He turns to another side of human nature which is often ignored. He assumes that men have a desire to be used for the service of their brethren and that men need to be needed. This is such a radical departure from the first appeal that we should look at it rather closely.

Consider, for example, the great civil rights movement of our day. It is not only our Negro brethren who are involved in it but thousands of white Americans who stand shoulder to shoulder beside them. When Martin Luther King sent out a call for help, preachers from all over the nation responded and went to Selma, Alabama, to march. Young men who could not afford the trip financially, found the money or took it from their savings and joined the march. One might have thought they would say that since they already have their civil rights, of what concern was it to them? But on the contrary, they felt that those who were denied these rights ought to have them, and they joined the struggle. To have asked these men to travel to Alabama for some personal gain would have left them unmoved. When, however, their witness was needed for the benefit of their brethren, they sacrificed to be with them.

Whenever a man gets involved in a reform movement, he is always disturbed at the connections entrenched evil has established with money and power. But he is also impressed with the number of people who have nothing to gain personally from the reform who will join his efforts because it is right. There seems to be in the heart of most of us a desire to stand by a man who is waging a brave battle for a good cause. There is much more of this in all of us than we realize.

In one of our church hospitals in a very exclusive suburban community, we have more women who have volunteered their service than we can possibly use. There is nothing to gain from their act so far as personal advantage is concerned, and there is certainly no prestige to be gained. But hundreds of well-to-do women both young and old stand ready to give time and energy to the sick just because they are told they are needed. When a young woman was doing a particularly dirty job, a society lady said, "I wouldn't do that for a thousand dollars." And the young woman glancing up replied, "Neither would I."

The man who travels widely will meet some discourtesies no doubt, but he will receive more kindness and help than he dared hope for. As I look back over the past years of my life and the many trips I have taken, I could spend a long time telling of the people who went out of their way to help me. I had no claim upon them at all, and often I could not even speak their language. But they took great pains to illuminate my darkness and set me on the right path.

My wife and I drove across the country in 1932 on our way to a theological seminary in Connecticut. It was our first long journey. We came into New York City late one night just as the theater crowd was filling the streets. This was my first experience in a city

like New York, and in a short while I was lost. I had to get through
New York, find the highway north and a motel that was inexpen-
sive. As I drew over to the curb with an apparently lost look on my
face, a car stopped. Three young men asked me what the trouble
was and I told them. I shall never forget how they said they would
be glad to show me the way through the city if I would but follow
them; and nearly an hour later, they waved me on my way. I like to
recall that incident when I read about teenage hoodlums.

I was trying to find my way through the intricacy of Rome a few
years ago and found myself coming back to the same place no
matter which turning I took. I tried to speak to a man passing by,
but he looked at me suspiciously. A little boy called out to him
something in Italian. Apparently he told him I was speaking
English and was lost. The man turned around, found a merchant
who could speak English and translate what my need was. Then
very carefully he drew a map, took me up to the corner, and pointed
out what I must do. I had no claim upon him except that I was in
trouble and needed help.

One of the big Detroit automobile companies hired a motivational
research organization to find out why so many people were buying
foreign cars. The interviewer spoke to a man who had purchased a
Volkswagen and asked him why. "That is easy," replied the VW
owner. "I felt it needed me." Ah, yes, we respond to need when we
deny the appeal to personal gain.

Now the third thing which Moses suggested to Hobab was that
they should

Do Something Together.

Moses' word was "And if you go with us, whatever good the Lord
will do to us, the same will we do to you."

We need one another and we need to be associated in a common
cause. Men who have gone through difficult times together find
values that are to be discovered in no other place. Remember the
words of Tom Paine about the testing of the Revolution, "These are
the times that try men's souls." Then he went on to talk about the

sunshine patriot and the summer soldier shrinking from the test. In a low moment of the Revolution, he brought new hope and new resolution. The nation was born out of men bound together in a hard and testing situation, and it was a great cause that gave them strength.

In the nineteenth century when Mazzini was trying to free Italy from outside invaders and internal tyrants, he sent out a call for volunteers. He promised them nothing but hard work and sacrifice, but the freedom of the nation was the goal. They came by the hundreds to enlist in a common enterprise full of danger and uncertainty. In 1941 a similar challenge was voiced by Winston Churchill, and it strengthened the English for their finest hour.

There seems to be an unwritten law of human nature that men become their best only when they are working together for something that is bigger than individual ambition. It is the big cause that fulfills man's need and dream. Let this be remembered in marriage, for two people who have nothing beyond themselves to hold them together and carry them onward will not go very far nor rise very high. A very wise Frenchman once said that being in love is not a matter of standing and gazing forever into each other's eyes, but of turning and looking together at the world.

It is this essential nature of the Church that we sometimes forget and it is a pity. I remember reading a book a long time ago that talked about three preachers who the author said symbolized three points of view of the ministry. One preacher went to his church and said in effect, "I am here for you to serve me." Strangely enough, said the writer, the church did just that, for they were proud of his ability and they carried him around on the shoulders of their administration. Anything he wanted they gave him, and they were happy to pay him a fine salary, give him time for travel or study, and seemed willing to exist as a congregation to glorify the pastor.

The second man came to his church and said in effect, "I am here to serve you." Interestingly enough, they were content to take him at his word. He became the errand boy of the church and did everything that any organization wanted done. If the women needed a man around to run some errands or to help arrange chairs and tables, he was there. If the young people needed a chauffeur to take them somewhere miles away, he played that part. His life from morning till night for seven days a week was at the beck and call of every group in the church.

But the writer described a third man who came to a church and said, "Let us together serve Christ." And that man understood the true nature of the ministry. He was not there to be served and he was not there to serve them, but he was there to call every member of that church to the common service of the Lord.

It has troubled me that men who have no time for church work, or at least so they say, will join a service club and put many hours of time on some community project. I have come to the conclusion that the fault is not theirs but ours. We have failed to make clear that the church is a company of men and women dedicated to the service of Christ and His Kingdom. It is for us to present to our people the big purpose and to hold before them the big demand, for only as we understand this shall we experience the big joy. The Christian church should be Moses telling every man that we are to go together and find our fulfillment in His service.

Some time ago I saw a statement from a preacher's wife which really surprised me. My amazement was even greater when I found out that she was the wife of an Anglican minister in England. This is what she said: "The clergy ought to be celibate because no decent, right-minded man ought to have the effrontery to ask any woman to take on such a lousy job! It is thoroughly unchristian." We must make allowances for a bad day, but still, there it is!

Only a fool will try to pretend that he knows what is in his wife's mind or try to speak for her on important matters. Yet I dare say that my wife would never say such a thing because she does not believe it. We have found that the ministry has been for us a binding together of our lives and the enlarging of our marriage. I am sorry for any couple who have not found a task in which they are involved completely.

Finally, we ought to note that

This Is the Way God Deals with Us.

His call is for participation in the common cause and for membership in His Kingdom. He comes to us as Moses came to Hobab with an invitation to go with Him and share with Him.

Here we run directly into the mystery of the love of God. It certainly is not an easygoing affection which always gives us what we want. It does not resemble some sentimental elder who wants to be sure that the young people have a good time. It is a strong, austere, and severe love which will lead us through suffering and pain. There is nothing sentimental about God's relationship with people.

Jesus gave us the clue to God's nature when he addressed Him as Father. There is no better word to express God's relationship with us. Fathers want the best for their children, but they are not willing to give it at the expense of character. The final desire is that the child may attain virtue and character rather than ease. When we talk about the Fatherhood of God we are talking about something so great that only our best and deepest human relations can give us a clue to it.

The final sign of what we are saying is the Cross. In spite of all appearances to the contrary, the Cross is God's word to men that He goes with them to the very end to redeem them and take them home. But it is a final word of hope and confidence that in our going with Him we shall never get beyond His care. It is here that we find the meaning of our life. It is here that we find ourselves a part of a mighty purpose that draws us close to one another and takes us into the presence of the Almighty. It is not an easy way and it has difficulties. But finally it is the joy we have of participating with God in the redemption of the world. And without this experience, life is never satisfactory or complete. He knows us better than we know ourselves.

Surely it is wonderful to think that our God does not seek to win our love by promising to do something for our advantage. He goes deeper than that and calls us by making us aware of the world's need and the world's pain. But best of all, we become a part of His process of healing.

The Fiji Islands were called originally The Cannibal Islands. They were inhabited by fierce and treacherous tribes whose main object was to kill and devour their enemies. John Hunt, a young Methodist missionary, went there many years ago. As a young man in England he was studying for the ministry and had just agreed to go to Africa as a missionary. He was engaged to a young woman who was willing to go with him, and what was more difficult, had obtained her mother's consent. Then the missionary society called him one day and told him that they wanted him to go to Fiji. John Hunt was willing but he wondered what Hannah would say. So he wrote her a letter and told her the change of plans and then waited for her answer. His friend saw how nervous he was and upset. Finally, John told him that he was unsure of Hannah. Then the letter came and with a shout John burst into his friend's room with the news. "It's all right," he said. "She says she will go with me anywhere."

Something like this happens to men who commit themselves to Jesus Christ and his Kingdom. Perhaps the most wonderful part of it all is the assurance that from that moment on, Christ will go with us wherever he wants us to go. It is this assurance that fills us with power and peace. We become partners with God in the tasks which He has to fulfill for our time.

❦ 6 ❧

Treasure in Earthen Vessels

> But we have this treasure in earthen vessels, to
> show that the transcendent power belongs to God
> and not to us.   II CORINTHIANS 4:7

THERE IS an old legend about the early days of the race when men gathered around the fire at night for protection and safety. They told stories about the events of the day and the experiences of the hunt. There was one member of the tribe who was not a good hunter and not a very skillful man in any of the common activities. But he had a great gift of words and he could tell stories about what had happened and the adventures his brethren had experienced. As they put it, "The words became alive and marched up and down in the hearts of the hearers." After a while some of the elders became concerned at the great power this man had with his words. "After we are gone," they said among themselves, "he may tell lies about us." So they killed him only to find when it was too late that the magic was not in the man but in the word.

Something of this recognition is being set forth to us in these words of St. Paul. He is saying to his generation and to ours that the magic is not in men. We are, he says, but earthen vessels, easily broken and not long-lasting. Anything we have of great value is from God who entrusts His treasures to our keeping for a while. The greatness of men, in other words, is not in themselves but in what they say, what they stand for, what they believe.

Until we come to terms with what men are, we are in no position to describe what we may expect from them. We have tended to neglect the Biblical anthropology while giving most of our attention to Biblical theology. This is not to say that we should neglect what we have done but that we must pay more attention to the Biblical word about man. If I were looking for a single statement which sums it up best, I would choose this affirmation of St. Paul. Here is the truth about man. Everything goes right with us if we remember it and everything goes wrong with us if we forget it. The evils of our time have their roots in a false interpretation of humanity, and until we can come to terms with the truth about human nature, all is in vain. Let us look with some care therefore at Paul's insight into the nature of man.

We may begin by suggesting that a great many people hope that

We Will Create a Race of Supermen.

This idea associated with Nietzsche is really rather commonplace in the thinking of our contemporaries. Just the other day I read of a scientist predicting we shall learn how to increase the size of our brain which will give us the ability to deal with the computer machines we are constructing. Our cry is for more intelligence, and we assume that if we could become smart enough we could solve our problems.

The literature written around the beginning to the French Revolution amazes us with its confidence in human reason. The Enlightenment was a hopeful move in the direction of salvation by brain. When we read some of the discourses set forth by eighteenth-century thinkers, we are amazed at their optimism and hope. They believed sincerely that once men were free from the shackles of class and allowed to follow their own bent without interference, they would create a heaven on earth. The natural goodness of humanity was lifted up to the exclusion of any recognition of sin and corruption, and it was bliss to be alive. What a terrible disillusionment it is to see the Revolution deteriorate into the Terror and become a pattern of madness more appropriate in an insane asylum than in a free nation.

In our time we have thought of science as the instrument which would set us free from limitations and mistakes. With the delicate instruments of precision we can do so many things and provide so many advantages. I read the other day that science has a machine which can weigh a book and measure the difference of five words. Surely this means science is the road to heaven.

In our own lifetimes we have gone from the hopefulness of scientific optimism to the pessimism of scientific despair. For out of this method and power have come the instruments of destruction and the threat of annihilation. Sometimes it seems as if in science we have a tiger by the tail dragging us over the brink, but we dare not let go. There was a day when men talked about a moratorium on preaching, and today there are many who secretly wish there could be a moratorium on science.

It is communist heresy which assumes that the new heaven and the new earth will come to us by way of intelligence. When Lenin and his followers cut themselves off from religion, they cut themselves off from the truth about human nature. They went back to the Enlightenment as the answer to human problems. Some of the books being smuggled out of Russia, which tell the story of life under the Soviets, do not seem to be descriptions of Utopia. The corruption of men is as apparent among communists as it is among capitalists.

Is it true that delinquency is simply a matter of underprivilege and poverty? Sometimes it is rooted in such things, but in our time our delinquents so often come from the right side of the avenue and from homes of overprivilege. We are wise when we try to fight poverty, but we are foolish if we think that the elimination of poverty means all will be well with us. One of the most disturbing things we face is bright young people with every material advantage who are morally sick.

My wife and I live up above the Hollywood Bowl and one summer Sunday morning passed the entrance to the Bowl on our way to a church where I was preaching. Young people were waiting at the gate which would not open until late afternoon. When we returned from church, we saw youngsters climbing around the hills above the Bowl, and cars were parked along roads too far away either to see or to hear what was going on. That night the Beatles arrived and now and again we could hear a great scream which sounded like nothing so much as a tribal frenzy being built up deliberately by a medicine man. What was going on? Four young men who need haircuts and have mildly pleasant voices were singing—or trying to; and I said to myself that it does not look as if this generation has made any notable progress toward solving their problems by intelligence.

The educated man is in a sense the real threat of our time. He is the one who has developed his brain and increased his intelligence until he can use crowds and concentrate power in himself. Whatever else may be said about dictatorship, it knows how to use brilliant men to create tyranny.

This must mean that there is a vast section of human life which education cannot reach. A man is not just a brain and a man is never entirely a rational creature. Those who think that bringing men into the Kingdom is merely a matter of increasing their thinking ability are on the wrong track. The education of the mind is important enough, but when the heart is left a jungle of primitive emotions, more education means more danger and a graver threat to the common life.

I must confess that I understand very little about the Laser beam. I know only that in some marvelous way it uses light to perform wonders of healing. It can be a weapon in man's fight against disease and darkness. But some time ago I saw that the Laser rifle can be used also to kill and destroy. And I thought to myself: Can it be true that light which symbolizes man's hope can actually be used as a weapon to destroy man? Apparently even light can be turned against man, and in some ways this is the greatest disillusionment of all. Those who believe that we can increase our intelligence and be saved by supermen are victims of a false hope and doomed to ultimate disillusionment.

We may move from this high concept and accept one which is too low. We can say that

Man Is Evil and Must Be Ruled.

Those who take this tack will say that men are little higher than the beasts and are victims of their wild, uncontrolled impulses. The answer is to recognize this and discipline men. Such men see freedom as an impossible idea and something which we do not want and are incapable of using wisely.

This, of course, is the fascist philosophy which we saw in action during World War II. When men saw what this means, they knew suddenly that this was not what they wanted. The heroism of the early forties was called to being by a vision of a nightmare world controlled for its own good by self-appointed masters.

We see the same philosophy at work in the economic exploitation of colonial peoples. The theory is that if people have not reached the proper level of culture and civilization, they must be ruled and used. Some of the strange antics of the newly free nations of Africa bear witness that it is a long road to self-discipline and self-control. Fascism may insist that certain races are innately inferior and must draw the water and hew the wood for the masters.

When this idea takes hold of men, it sometimes turns even great scholars into propagandists. Professor William Albright, the famous archeologist, points out that such a tragedy overcame two German scholars, Kittel and Fischer. Fischer was a scientist, an authority on human genetics, and Kittel was a leading Protestant scholar and theologian. These two men, captured by the dream of national socialism in Germany, deserted their scholarly discipline and collaborated on a book which brought blushes to the cheeks of every scholar in the field. Listen to these words of Albright:

In many ways Kittel and Fischer typified European intellectual activity at its best, since the two men were leaders in their philological and biological fields. Surrendering to the devil of intellectual overconfidence, they plunged into the uncharted depths between their respective islands of special skill. Selling themselves to satan, they abandoned the Judeo-Christian tradition of the fatherhood of God and the brotherhood of man. Worshipping at the shrine of the ancient pagan gods of *Blut und Boden,* they adopted the mark of Cain as their perpetual badge of dishonor. And what happened in Germany can take place wherever the human intellect turns its back on the spiritual traditions which we have inherited from their sources in ancient Israel.*

Thus did these scholars sell themselves to men seeking some intellectual excuse to persecute the Jews.

This same danger is manifest when men distrust the physical part of life. Sometimes in the name of a superior spirituality, they regard the body as intrinsically evil and adopt the Greek doctrine of body and spirit in constant inevitable warfare. St. Paul pictured the body as the temple of the Holy Spirit, and only when we remember this truth can we remain healthy.

If sex is regarded as an evil thing in itself, then the monasteries become centers of a superior religious experience because marriage is repudiated. Sex that is thus repressed breaks out every now and again in evil excesses because it is one of the powerful impulses God has given men. The Biblical teaching is that all of life is sacred. Whenever we despise a part of it, we have failed to understand the truth about ourselves.

There was a small fundamentalist college somewhere in the Middle West that advertised it was seven miles from any known form of sin. If I could believe that there was any place I could go that would get me seven miles away from sin, I would go there as fast as possible. I would apply for a job on the faculty of such a college, and if refused, I would be glad to be a caretaker. But, of course, this is all nonsense. If it is true that man is not above all evil, it is true also that he cannot live his life by subjugating any impulse that may lead to evil.

* William Foxwell Albright, *History, Archeology and Christian Humanism,* McGraw-Hill, 1964.

Paul's word is that

Man's Treasure Is in Earthen Vessels.

He may roam the heavens, but his feet are made of clay. He is capable of the best and of the worst, and in his person he bears the mark of greatness and the stain of depravity.

This means, I think, that man is a symbol of something both a part of him and beyond him. The significant thing about us is what we believe. There was a time when we suggested that it makes no difference what we believe just so we are sincere. We were looking not only for a religionless Christianity but a creedless Christianity. All of this is nonsense, for we are shaped and our destiny is determined by what we dare to believe.

On Sunday morning in most churches there is a time when the congregation stands together and repeats the creed. It may be a modern affirmation of faith or the Apostles' Creed. We do it perfunctorily usually, but this is one of the great moments of worship and one of the great experiences in human life. When a congregation stands and says "I believe in God the Father Almighty, Maker of heaven and earth," that is a great moment. For in that act we confess our allegiance to something beyond the world and to One whose ways are not our ways. Only man can do this and only man can proclaim faith in values far beyond himself.

Our greatness comes out of what we stand for. How often I have seen this in my ministry. I look at ordinary people without exceptional gifts whose lives have become symbols of the undying and the everlasting. This is what Paul was talking about when he wrote to the Ephesians, "Therefore take the whole armor of God, that you may be able to withstand in the evil day, and having done all, to stand" (6:13). We may be earthen vessels, indeed, but we have been given the power to incarnate greatness.

Our nature is determined by what and by whom we serve. If we bear the sign of the King, it marks us as creatures who bear eternal treasure within earthen vessels. This came to me a few years ago when I met an elderly bishop of our church. After years of service in Africa, he retired in this country and attended the meetings of our Council. He had a tendency to wander a bit when he spoke, and there was nothing in his words of drama or excitement. And then I went to Africa myself and my eyes were opened. I learned how years ago this man and his wife had walked the trails up through the Congo jungle. I went to small villages where an old man or an old woman would inquire through the interpreter if I knew Bishop Springer. Then they would tell about how young Dr. Springer had come there years ago and told the story of his Master. It came to me that this man was full of wonder and light because he had dedicated his service to Christ. Treasure in an earthen vessel, indeed!

This is a Christian paradox which in some ways is very confusing to the world. For on the one hand, the Christian is haughtier than all others and takes a higher point of view toward himself and his brethren. Then just as we are getting ready to talk about Christian pride, we see in him the humbleness and humility that come from a frank recognition of his own sins and mistakes. The Christian is very humble about himself and very proud of what he represents and whom he serves.

There is no wailing sadness in the Christian about man. You will find the Christian discouraged about his own sins at times and weeping over his own unworthiness. But about man who has been made a little lower than the angels, he takes a very high view and will insist that no man is to be treated as less than a son of God.

The Christian will not believe that all evil is appearance and he will not believe in a superior knowledge that sets him above evil. He must on the contrary keep clear in his mind that evil is real enough and succeeds too often in overcoming good human impulses. But he keeps coming back to the insight of St. Paul that this earthen vessel is worthy of honor because it contains a divine treasure.

One of my friends, the late Dr. Roy L. Smith, said that he went to college by a great sacrifice of his parents. He had won the broad jump in a track meet that first year, and when he came home, this was all he could talk about. In vain his mother tried to find out what he had learned and what new ideas had come to him. But all he could do was boast of his athletic victory. One day as they rode together out across the Kansas prairie, a jack rabbit came out of a bush, ran across the road, and disappeared. His mother said quietly, "Roy, that jack rabbit never went to college and it can jump farther than you can." Roy Smith got the point and realized that college was not primarily to make him an athlete but to do something for his mind and his spirit. Physically, we are but earthen vessels, but spiritually, we can contain the eternal treasures of God.

Finally, let us rejoice that

God Triumphs Through Our Weaknesses.

It is good news for ordinary folks that some of the greatest treasures have come from very plain vessels. Rabbi Joshua was once taunted by an emperor's daughter because of his mean appearance. He pointed to the earthen jars which contained her father's finest wines. Whereupon she placed the wine in silver vessels, but it turned sour. The rabbi then taught her that humble vessels sometimes contain the greatest treasure.

I think of the young woman who will never be Miss California or Miss America or Miss Universe. In spite of TV's propaganda that nothing can happen to the girl who has not learned all the beauty tricks, life is still more than a surface prettiness. She may find the inner beauty which increases with every passing year. She may learn a happiness deeper than the poor young woman who thinks that the earthen vessel is all there is to it. Or here is the young man who will never be in the movies. No one will ever ask him to model for a shirt, but let him learn that God has great treasure to bestow upon any man who can accept it.

This is the meaning of the Incarnation. Isaiah spoke of the Man of Sorrows acquainted with grief. He wrote about One who had no comeliness and from whom people would turn their faces. Let us never forget the mystery and the wonder of God coming to us through a man. And what a man he was! Tempted as we are tempted and treated not as royalty but as scum, he was denied the ordinary securities of life and knew little about the comforts of living. Finally, he died in anguish and pain to say to us that these earthen vessels we call our bodies reflect the glory of God. Martin Luther had the courage to suggest that each man could be an incarnation and ought to be as Christ to his neighbor. This is good news.

An American was worshiping one Sunday morning in one of the largest Protestant churches of Dresden in East Germany. He reports that during the service he was astonished to hear the pastor pray for the mayor of Dresden, the district governor of Saxony, and the head of the East German regime—all communists. After the service he wanted to ask about it. The pastor reminded him gently that St. Paul in the Book of Romans exhorts Christians to pray for their rulers who were persecuting them and would one day execute St. Paul. "And besides," the pastor said quietly, "when I pray for the mayor it reminds him that he is not God."

Oh, let no man believe that he can become wise enough to be a god. Let us never be corrupted by the teaching that some men are to be ruled and used by wiser men. But let us rejoice in St. Paul's word that we have treasure in earthen vessels and remember who we are. For in this word there is our salvation and our joy.

❦ 7 ❧

In the Name of the Lord

> Then David said to the Philistine "You come to me with a sword and with a spear and with a javelin; but I come to you in the name of the Lord of hosts. . . ." I SAMUEL 17:45

THE STORY is one of the best known and the most popular in the Bible. Since our Sunday School days we have heard about David and Goliath, and it is one of the favorite tales of the Old Testament. It will need only a brief sketching.

The army of Philistia was encamped on one hilltop and across the valley was the army of Israel. But the Philistines had a mighty man of valor who came out every day and taunted the Israelites to send a champion against him. Whoever won the personal combat would decide the national issue. But Israel had no champion who could stand against this mighty giant encased in armor and carrying a spear "like a weaver's beam." Day followed day and the morale of the Israelites was at an all-time low.

Into the situation there came a shepherd boy named David. His father had sent him down from Bethlehem with some special food for three of his brothers who were fighting in the army of Israel and with a gift to present to the commander. He was to bring back news of the battle to his father. When David heard Goliath's taunt, he volunteered to go against him, but King Saul was reluctant to send him. However, since there was no one else, the king agreed finally that he could go and outfitted him with his own armor. But it did not fit and David cast it aside. Picking up five smooth stones from the brook, he took his sling and went forth to meet the arrogant Philistine.

Goliath was more amused than angry and he cursed the shepherd boy. Then David replied, "You come to me with a sword and with a spear and with a javelin; but I come to you in the name of the Lord of hosts, the God of the armies of Israel, whom you have defied." Fitting a stone into his sling, he threw it at Goliath, pierced his forehead and killed him. What I want us to think about for a little while is the great affirmation of David: "I come to you in the name of the Lord of hosts."

Let us begin with the observation that

Goodness Always Seems Weaker than Evil.

Here in miniature is the constant struggle always going on between sin and virtue. Indeed Arnold Toynbee uses this story as an illustration of a principle of history in *A Study of History*. He says that it is an analogue of the biological competition between the tiny soft man against the massive armored reptile. In military history we see how heavy armor is brought down by a more mobile, adjustable force. It is the swift, maneuverable, small English ships that outsail the galleons of the Spanish Armada.

Still, there are many who doubt this affirmation and insist that safety lies only in the large armament. Napoleon said that God fights on the side of the big battalions. and he intimated that if you wish to know who will win, find out who has the most men and the thickest steel. But when Victor Hugo wrote about the battle of Waterloo in his classic *Les Misérables,* he expressed quite a different point of view. He asked if it were possible for Napoleon to have won that battle and he answered no. Not because of Blücher or of Wellington but because of God, said Hugo. Napoleon, he declared, embarrassed God. That I suppose is the perfect answer to the man who said that the big battalions are the guarantee of victory.

Through nineteen centuries the Church has been David against the Goliath of the world. People seldom take it very seriously, and so far as its strength is concerned, they are likely to ask Stalin's question about the Pope's strength: "How many battalions does he have?" Yet Hitler was not the first dictator and in all probability will not be the last to be surprised by the strength of the Church which has seemed so weak. For when the crisis comes, there has been an unseen spiritual power possessed by the church which has brought down tyranny. As James Russell Lowell put it in "The Present Crisis," if right is on the scaffold and wrong is on the throne, still it is the scaffold that sways the future. We believe that God stands in the shadows keeping watch.

We see it happen in scenes close to home. The reformer is usually David, and the entrenched evil of the community is Goliath. A man knows something is wrong and begins the attack to discover that corruption has powerful political and financial connections greater than he thought. It can always call on resources not available to reform, and yet, the reformer finds power men did not imagine was available. Every change in society for the good has been against an enemy that seemed invincible.

Remember that when the spies came back from the Promised Land and reported to Moses, only two of them believed that Israel could possess the land. They said that if God had promised it to them, He would help them take it, and they advised going up immediately. Ten of the spies, however, were sure that it could not be done, and the people listened to the majority report, which is not always wise. So Israel wandered for a generation in the wilderness, doubting that a David could overcome a Goliath.

We talk about the mystery of suffering, for it is beyond our understanding and no man can explain it. We talk about the difficulty of evil fitting into a universe where a good God rules. But to me there is a greater mystery, which is the persistence of goodness and the inability of evil finally to overcome it. Why does not the time come when we give up all hope and confess that decency has been exterminated at last and violence has won an ultimate victory? Believe me, the whole history of man is full of this mystery. David listens to the taunt of Goliath for just so long and then moves against him. Mankind never accepts wrong as having won the final victory, and that is a very great mystery indeed.

Teilhard de Chardin wrote *The Phenomenon of Man,* in my mind one of the great books of our generation. He was a Catholic priest forbidden to publish the results of his scholarship and research during his lifetime. Unable to share his conclusions, yet he was never despondent and always had a remarkable joy about him. Asked one time why he was happy, he gave the strange reply, "Because the earth is round." What did he mean, do you suppose? Perhaps that all mankind belongs together and can never be separated finally and perhaps that there is something in the nature of the world to bring us closer together as a family. So it is that the religious man finds a basis for hope and courage. Life never becomes easy nor is the triumph of goodness ever provable. But men rejoice because of this mystery of goodness by which we are able to believe that at the end of the day, David defeats Goliath.

Another truth that comes from this story is that

Man Is Not Self-Sufficient.

The strength of Goliath was only in himself, and his pride betrayed him. David proclaimed that he came in the power of a mighty faith.

We live in what might be called the psychological age. Its jargon becomes a part of our vocabulary, and although we do not always know the accurate meaning of terms, we use them glibly. Every man is an expert in analyzing what's wrong with everybody else or with himself, and the answer to inner conflict is to be found on the couch in the psychoanalyst's office.

All of this we accept gladly, for we have learned much about the workings of the human mind through psychiatry. There is, however, one fundamental weakness which needs to be noticed, and it takes great courage to point it out. Criticizing theology or philosophy is commonplace, but psychology has become our sacred cow. Yet it must be said that much psychology assumes that man's problems can be solved from within himself and through his own wisdom. It assumes that man is self-sufficient and that by proper adjustment he can live happily and successfully. With this point of view religion finds no agreement. The values which give meaning to life are not merely subjective. This is the fundamental difference between religion and psychology, and we have done neither of these disciplines any favor by pretending that it does not exist. From my point of view, only when the psychologist is at the same time a religious man can he bring an ultimate healing to a sick soul.

At the present time there is a struggle going on between the humanities and science. When the Russians launched their first sputnik, it frightened us and suddenly we feared that our survival was at stake. Everything that taught us how to produce engineers and scientists became good, and everything that did not contribute to that main purpose was looked upon as secondary and unimportant. We must survive at all costs, we believe, but there is another question that is beginning to intrude upon our minds. It is whether or not we are the kind of creatures that are worthy of survival.

Is the pursuit of beauty and truth and meaning merely an extra in our lives which we can dismiss in a time of crisis? Are these just options with no practical value? Is what we used to call the liberal arts an elective in the curriculum? When man makes survival his only aim, he tends to become merely a clever, thinking animal. But a man is more and these pursuits and achievements which lead us beyond ourselves prove to be essentials.

We have done much to improve our physical lot and life gets easier for us every year. It is a nuisance to wind your watch, and now we make them self-winding to relieve us of that chore. While the TV commercials spend all kinds of money to tell us that brushing our teeth is important, we ought not to be expected to put forth any effort so we invent electric toothbrushes. Who wants to crank up the windows of his car when he can have an electric switch do it with a touch? Yet, all of this so-called progress is merely making life easier, and it does not seem to make life richer or more satisfactory. Indeed, the farther we go along this path, the more boredom and despair seem to be waiting for us at the end of the road.

Our times encourage us to be self-centered and to massage our own egos. Of course, the Bible has warned us against this and Jesus said bluntly that if a man wants to gain his life he must be willing to lose it. The Bible, however, is an old book and for many of us, out of date. Yet, strangely enough, even the psychology which we regard so highly tells us the same thing. The man who walks through an endless hall of mirrors looking at himself and thinking of himself is on the way to insanity. We seem to need a goal beyond ourselves in order to live with any satisfaction.

We pretend sometimes that we can trust only ourselves. I met a Frenchman not long ago in the Middle East who told me that De Gaulle's prayer every morning is "O Lord, trust me." Well, it is not only De Gaulle who prays that prayer, and this is a part of the trouble that overtakes us. Only a fool can believe that he is completely trustworthy. We say things we should not have said and we do things which we should not have done. Sometimes when a great disaster overtakes us, we are crushed by the knowledge that we were our own betrayers. The foundation upon which I stand with certainty and courage is never my own trustworthiness.

On some university campuses we have seen demonstrations and sit-ins for various causes. Not always has there been a real issue at stake, but young people, soon or late, need to announce their allegiance to something beyond themselves. This generation has been called selfish and uninvolved, but it breaks forth every now and again in a demonstration for civil rights or for integration or for justice. We do not find that preparation for our own careers and studying to make ourselves successful represents enough to live for. Humanity may get weary of ideals and dedicate itself to selfish values alone. Soon or late, however, it never works and we are face to face with the truth that until we have found something to serve unselfishly, we have not found the clue to life.

A Scottish shepherd one time said that sheep caught in a blizzard can live for seven or eight days by eating their own wool. But at the end of that time, they will freeze to death. That, my brethren, is a parable. We can feed upon ourselves and be concerned only with ourselves for a time, but there is no lasting answer in that process. Goliath represents those who glory in their own strength and their own success but discover finally that it does not save them.

The third thing we ought to consider is that

Our Meaning Is Beyond Ourselves.

To put it another way, man is a symbol of something eternal. He cannot be confined to the cultivation of only human values. He has to walk the earth, but he is also a creature of heavenly aspirations and hopes.

Man is a listener to voices one of which seems to speak from some inner depth. We call it conscience. All of my life I have heard men try to explain this phenomenon in such a way as to make it definable. There have been those who suggested that it is nothing much more than a bad case of indigestion or perhaps our glands are out of order. We are told that it is simply the result of what our parents have taught us and oftentimes they were wrong. None of this really explains anything, for we know that the inner voice is the real Mt. Sinai of our lives from whence come the commandments. We obey our conscience and find happiness, or deny it and find only misery. As Viktor Frankl has said, "Conscience is the voice of transcendence; man intercepts the voice but does not originate it."

There is a voice from without which says with special insistence that no man is an island and no man lives unto himself. I stood one day at the Memorial of Witness and Warning in Jerusalem and saw a photograph of little children being herded toward the gas ovens in one of Hitler's concentration camps. It was such a horrible thing that it almost made me ill. Then I said to myself, "Why should you be so concerned? You never knew those children. You do not know who their parents were. Why are you so upset by what happened to perfect strangers?" The answer is, of course, that no man is a perfect stranger and no child is beyond my responsibility. Somehow I was part of the civilization that performed that crime, and I had a deep sense of guilt. Strange, indeed, that the voice that speaks to us from without speaks about unknown men and carries such authority.

There is, of course, the Voice that speaks from above and seems to come to us directly from God. Isaiah heard it in the day of his disappointment when he went into the temple. It was a voice asking for a messenger, and he found his peace when he replied, "Here am I! Send me." It is my conviction that until a man says yes to these voices beyond himself, he does not find life.

This is the testimony of David who came to represent his people. But he was representing a people who had signed a contract with God and made an agreement with the Most High. He did not come in his own name, and he was representing more than himself. The greatness of Israel was its realization that they lived their lives and fought their battles in the name of God.

This affirmation is the important testimony which comes out of this story. Nations and people live by loyalties to something beyond themselves, and so do individuals. Woe unto that man who is committed only to his own success and struggles only for the attainment of his own purposes. Soon or late he meets somebody who comes against him with a larger loyalty, and then he knows how poor he is and how inadequate his purpose. For every man there comes a time when he must ask himself in all seriousness in whose name he is living.

Some time ago I was invited to Asbury Theological Seminary, and I read about the founding of the school before I went to the campus. Henry Clay Morrison started the college from which came the theological siminary. He writes about the time he received his local preacher's license, which is the first step in The Methodist Church toward becoming a Methodist minister. The meeting was held in a little Kentucky church, and one of the items of business was whether or not to recommend Henry Morrison to the quarterly conference to be licensed as a local preacher. When the vote was taken it was all yes except one no from his half-brother Tom. On the road home that night, Tom was bitter. He told Henry that if he had known what was coming up, he would have taken steps to prevent it from happening. He said that Henry had no gifts for the ministry, and if there was one thing he could not stand it was a second-rate Methodist preacher dragging his half-starved family around from appointment to appointment. He said to Henry, "I stand in with the congressman of this district and I could have gotten you into West Point and made an army officer out of you, or I could have put you with Judge Durham in Danville to make a lawyer out of you. You could have been somebody of whom we would feel proud." By this time young Henry was weeping, and he said, "But, Tom, you see the Lord has called me to preach." To which Tom only answered, "He must be hard up for material."

Oh, think of all the poor young men who have been called to some great job and found that it made them strong. Think of all the inadequate men who have obeyed a voice beyond themselves and it directed them to great achievement. There is nothing more wonderful than to see a life that might have been mediocre grow great with a commission bestowed upon it from God.

Finally, let us note that there is

Power in Religious Faith.

No one does very much until he believes, and nothing becomes irresistible until it is undergirded by faith.

The great generation always believes, and the poor generation is governed by its doubts. The great thing about America in 1776 was a mighty achievement in the name of freedom and equality. The poor thing about America in 1965 is its lack of faith in its heritage and its loss of hope in its future.

Methodism is an example of a movement that grows strong with its belief and weak from its doubt. The early Methodist preachers were not as well trained nor as able as our modern preachers. Oftentimes they were laymen who only had an experience to proclaim. One of the reasons they moved to new circuits very often was their lack of ability to preach with freshness in the same place for any length of time. It was their faith that made them great and effective. With all the substitutes we have found, such as institution, wealth, and numbers, the essential thing about a church is a vital sense of living its life in the name of Christ. In one of the early meetings of the Methodists in New York, a man in the uniform of a captain in the British army came in and sat in the back. The people were nervous because some of their preachers had been impressed and some soldiers had tried to break up previous meetings. They went through the service anxiously, and after the benediction, the British captain stood up, came down to the front of the room, and announced, "I am Captain Thomas Webb of the King's Service and also a soldier of the Cross and a spiritual son of John Wesley." He became one of the most generous and diligent early members of the church, and I have thought often of that moment when he announced himself as a man not only serving in the name of the king but in the name of the King of Kings and one of his greatest servants, John Wesley.

Find a man who has been ordained a servant of God and discover the depth of his life and the power of his witness compared with the man who lives only for himself. So the story of David and Goliath is repeated over many times in each generation, and men with only the natural endowments of birth, power, and wealth find themselves no match for men who rise up in the name of God.

For two thousand years we have been using the phrase, "In the name of Jesus Christ." It is in these words that we find the power of the Christian church, and in that confession there is the strength of each Christian man. For at long last God came to us through our Lord and bestowed upon us the name that is above every name and before whom the devils tremble.

It is reported that when Gertrude Stein was dying in Paris, some of her friends stood about her bed. She opened her eyes and asked, "What is the answer?" There was no reply because they did not know the answer any more than she did. "Well, then," she asked, "what is the question?" Those were her last words. I do not know many answers any more than you do, but I am sure I know the question: In whose name do we live? Once we have found the right question, Christians also know the answer. There is a name that is power and victory and joy. It is Jesus Christ.

❦ 8 ❧

Concerning Peace of Mind

Come to me, all who labor and are heavy laden,
and I will give you rest.   MATTHEW 11:28

In 1946, Rabbi Joshua Liebman of Boston wrote a book called *Peace
of Mind*. I was one of the few not much impressed with it, but it
caught on and became a bestseller. The title is a part of this generation's vocabulary. There were preachers who said this was the heart
of religion, and their message was centered around this main theme.
There were others who said such preaching was a travesty of the
message of the Gospel, and such an emphasis was sub-Christian.
Many laymen have heard the peaceful message gladly but many
preachers have found it theologically wanting.

One thing perfectly clear is that many people in our time live
under tension and know trouble. Any man who can promise them
relaxation and give them a cure for insomnia is heard gladly. Books
on the subject are legion. Life is hard for most of us, and with all
our progress we have not found it easier to live at ease with ourselves in our world.

What I would like to do is examine this concept and ask the
extent to which it is legitimate. I want to look at God's promises in
the Bible. Especially I want Jesus' light on this dark subject. So I
have chosen a text in which he seems to promise exactly what the
Jewish rabbi promised and what some of our popular preachers

promise. Jesus says, "Come to me, all who labor and are heavy laden and I will give you rest." He seems to be saying that he will give the weary relief and he will set us free from our burdens.

Let me begin with the proposition that in any case

We Are Not Supposed to Have It All the Time.

This is probably the main mistake we make. If it is good, why not now? If it is enjoyable now, why not always?

Society hopes for a state free from conflict or danger. We feel that if we could only eliminate the racial strife with its accompanying sit-ins and protest marches, we would be at ease. What a fine condition we would be in if there were no strikes and no conflict between management and labor! The quiet society appears to be the perfect society, and we would attain it if we could. Actually, such a condition would be the next thing to death.

A church gets uneasy when it has financial problems or tension within its fellowship. Many a member thinks the ideal arrangement would be a church without debt or burdens. We would like to find a preacher whom everybody admired and nobody criticized. Struggles in the church seem to many people a sure sign that all is not well, and they seek peace as the most desirable of all goals.

Men who are going through trouble long for the time when they may be relieved of all problems. A man may think that retirement will be the solution of all his problems. If we can get out from underneath the responsibilities life has put upon us, we think we can live in a happy state forever. Yet, one of my laymen who retired comparatively young with an adequate income, said to me not long ago, "Can you help me find something to do? I am getting so tired of just playing golf." Imagine!

We forget that life is contrast and that one continual mood is monotonous. Jesus makes this plain when he gives us the Beatitudes as descriptions of blessedness. What kind of sense does it make to be told that we are to find happiness from being hungry or thirsty or persecuted for righteousness' sake? Yet Jesus knew that a life of constant relaxation would be just another name for hell.

Look at it from the physical standpoint. It is a great pleasure to eat a good meal when you are hungry. But it is not much fun to eat when you are not hungry, and appetite is created by putting forth effort and hard work. The rich man who has lost his appetite would give anything for the hunger he knew when he was young and poor. The truth seems to be that enjoyment comes after strenuous effort and hard labor.

In the mental and spiritual realms, the truth is just the same. A lady once said to a writer that she supposed he enjoyed writing. He replied, "Madam, writers do not enjoy writing. They only enjoy having written." Quite so! Not many preachers will tell you it is fun to prepare sermons, and the older I grow, the more it becomes pain and woe. I run more scared with every passing year. But if the preparation has been hard and arduous, the joy comes in delivering a message which you know is your best.

Let us look at the text again. Jesus does not say "Come unto me all you who have been loafing." He does not say "Come unto me all you who have refused to get involved in anything risky." He says that we may come to him for rest if we have been working hard and that we may find strength in him if we have borne heavy burdens. His promise is rest after toil and peace out of struggle.

A perfect example of peace of mind, I think, is a cow standing in the shade of a tree in a pleasant meadow on a summer day chewing her cud. If you have ever watched such a creature gazing out across the field with vacant eyes, you must have felt that here is the perfect picture of contentment and ease. But if I were asked to give an example of man at his best, it would be Sir Wilfred Grenfell risking his life daily as he ministered to the sick of Labrador and saying that he never had made a sacrifice in his life. Or I would think of Albert Schweitzer and his demonstration of love and concern at primitive Lambaréné when he could have been enjoying the culture and acclaim of Europe for his brilliance. I would think of Jeremiah speaking a bitter word that he did not want to speak and cursing the day he was born. Said Oliver Wendell Holmes, Sr.: "The longing for certainty and repose is in every human mind. But certainty is generally illusion and repose is not the destiny of man."

The second thing we ought to say is that

Peace of Mind Is a By-product.

It does not come to men who seek it, and those who find it never exactly know how or when or why.

What I am talking about is a perfect example of serendipity. That is a word that many people like me will have to look up in a dictionary. But it is an important word and it describes a true insight into the nature of our life. There is an old legend of three princes of Seredip, which is the ancient name for Ceylon. Wherever they went they never found what they were seeking, but they found something better. Sir Horace Walpole, writing to a friend in 1754, commented on the story and coined this word—serendipity. It means finding something unexpectedly, greater than the thing which you were seeking consciously. It means experiencing something which could never have been found unless we were seeking something else.

The truth is that life always goes out beyond our logic. There is always an untamed element that will not be controlled by reason. We do our best to turn psychology and sociology into sciences, but we do not succeed and God willing we never shall succeed. For there is always the unexpected, and life never yields itself completely to laws of cause and effect.

Christianity understands this and Jesus announced great paradoxes. He tells us that if we want to find something, we have to lose it, which is not logical but is grandly true. He speaks to us of the joy of sacrifice and of the happiness of service. He talks about the divine surprises in life which come to those who choose his way. He never offered man ease, but he promised a strange, almost absurd kind of joy if we set our minds on seeking the Kingdom of God.

There are some things which are not proper human goals, and peace of mind is one of them. If you want to be sure that you will never know it, then make finding it the purpose of your life. The men I know who are at ease with themselves and their world are men who are caught up in viable causes and say yes to duty. The unhappiest people I meet are those who have nothing else to do except to seek ease and give all their life in its vain pursuit.

Happiness cannot come to us through any direct action. Charles Schulz, who has given us *Peanuts,* makes this clear when he says that happiness is a warm puppy, or happiness is winning an argument with your sister, or happiness is knowing the answer in school. It is something that comes only when we are not seeking it.

There are those who believe that to keep uninvolved in people's troubles makes happiness. We are so afraid of being taken in, as we say, so we make up our minds to stand apart from other people's anxieties. Well, we have our wish, and instead of being taken in, we are left out altogether. Instead of finding happiness, we find misery.

Cleveland Amory was traveling in Maine shortly after the national election and asked an old lady how she voted. She answered, "I didn't vote. It only encourages them." But we do not find any peace of mind by staying aloof or refusing to share in the common life. All such deliberate attempts to preserve our peace of mind can lead only to disaster.

The third thing I want to say is that we are living fully only when we are

Being Used by a Mighty Purpose.

Nobody has said this quite so clearly and satisfactorily as George Bernard Shaw. We could not call him an orthodox Christian, but I have always felt he was a deeply religious man. He wrote, "This is the true joy of life, the being used for a purpose recognized by yourself as a mighty one; the being thoroughly worn out before you are thrown out on the scrap heap; the being a force of nature instead of a feverish, selfish little clod of ailments and grievances complaining that the world will not devote itself to making you happy."

Life goes wrong when we make trivial what ought to be great, and we have a gift for making great things trivial. Consider television. It is hard for me to realize that it was born and developed in the last few years of my own life. We bought our first television set in 1952. When I consider its miracle, I am almost overwhelmed. Think of bringing into my living room the events that are going on thousands of miles away! Now that Telstar has been launched, think of what it will mean to have the events from all over the world brought before our eyes in our own homes! But when programs are interspersed with tasteless commercials which are trying to sell deodorants or cigarettes, the whole miracle of television becomes cheap and tawdry. When we think of what it could be and what the hucksters have made of it, we should weep.

G. K. Chesterton visited New York years ago, and when he saw Times Square at night he made a very strange remark. "What a place this would be for a man who could not read," he said. I suppose he meant that the miracle of moving light is most impressive until you realize it is just a means to sell motor cars and whiskey. Or if you go to Las Vegas as I do, and I hasten to add I go there to preach, you will find two blocks downtown which are even brighter than Times Square. Out on the Strip spectacular electric displays stand in front of the casinos with breath-taking beauty. But when you remember that all this is to lure people into gambling halls, it makes it all look cheap and disappointing. Watch the gamblers in the morning haggard, sad, and despondent, and the glamor becomes ashes.

Look at the great professions! There is medicine which calls for the complete dedication of a man's life and skill to healing and ministering to the sick. But a man may turn this profession into merely a financial proposition. He may operate only if he receives his fee and refuse to be concerned if a man is poor. He may agree to see some anxious, terrified soul if he can get to his office during office hours, but have no ear for a sudden cry at midnight. Medicine can become just a way of making a good living and nothing more.

Or there is the law. I have said to some of my lawyer friends that they are in a position to minister to men in a way that makes their work a ministry. Nobody goes to a lawyer unless he is in trouble, and for the man who sees the law as a profession of service, there are countless opportunities to help people when they really need it. But a man can also become an ambulance chaser or a shyster and turn the profession into the comparatively trivial business of making money.

Even the ministry can become merely a way of earning a living. There is, unfortunately, no guarantee that a man who enters the service of the Church will escape the temptation to make his calling something selfish and sordid. There are not many such ministers, but I have known a few.

America needs a new vision of itself and its destiny. We fall too much under the influence of men who encourage us to keep what we have and deny it to those seeking a new and better life. Whether it be our immigration policy or our foreign aid, our temptation is to forget that under God we are called not only to protect our investments but to demonstrate freedom. Our task is to be the servant nation bringing encouragement to all peoples who are struggling to attain a better society.

While traveling in the Middle East some time ago, I stopped one day at the old Roman city of Jerash in Syria. It was one of the three or four great Roman cities of its time and enough of it has been restored to give the visitor an idea of its splendor. There is a great long way lined with columns, a large amphitheater on the hill, and the remains of beautiful temples of worship. There was another man there at the same time, and he was carrying a transistor radio with some loud music blaring from a nearby radio station. The mood of wonder at the greatness of the past was dissipated, and I walked through the grandeur that was Roman culture forced to listen to a cheap contribution from my own civilization. And I thought again of how we can take the greatest experience and make it something vulgar and noisy.

There is a sense in which the Church exists to remind us who we are and what our purposes should be. Noisy living and trivial thinking corrodes the dignity of our status as the sons of God. But as we come together to worship and serve in the name of Christ, we see once again God's plan for us and God's call to greatness.

We are engaged in a real struggle and there are real issues at stake. We may pretend that all of this is empty idealism, but once we deny it, everything goes wrong with us. Life is an adventure when the purposes are big, and I find contentment in my soul only when I am serving an important enterprise.

A man was registering in a hotel in Acapulco just as a rich American was checking out. The big spender paused for a moment in the lobby and began counting the money in his wallet. After he had finished, he said in a surprised tone, "I am not spending enough money. I must not be having very much fun." Such a life will produce no peace of mind.

Finally, we come to the glad realization that

The Gospel Promises a New and Lasting Experience of Peace.

It does not bring us what some people think they want because the Christian faith is wiser than our philosophy. It understands us better than we understand ourselves, and its reward of inner joy comes to us by a rather strange route.

The Gospel meets us with high demands for service and sacrifice. We start with the Cross and we must never forget it, although we are surrounded by sects which ignore it. You may be sure when the Cross is not the center of the teaching, that religion is false in spite of its use of Christian terms. This symbol of our faith is the sign of defeat and a reminder of the worst thing that could happen to the human race. This is where it begins, and to a good many people it does not seem to be possible that such a beginning could lead to "peace of mind."

Jesus never said to his followers, "Now, fellows, just do the best you can. God will understand that not too much can be expected of you." On the contrary, he comes to say to us, "Be perfect as your heavenly Father is perfect." There seems to be precious little peace of mind in that demand.

He never intimates that we are to live on an easy basis without discipline. On the contrary, he talks about life being constantly under judgment and commands us to be accountable at any moment. He talks about the seriousness of each day's happenings and about our responsibility for every careless word we speak. This does not sound like the way of relaxation and ease.

But as we begin here we come to the promise of help and of power not our own. We are to extend ourselves in such a way that we cannot do it by ourselves, and we are to live by our faith in God. Jesus talks about evil and promises us forgiveness of our sins. He speaks of weakness but he promises strength for our labor. He calls to all those who carry big loads and promises them rest and refreshment.

It is faith that we live by and it is faith that is our strength. We follow him not to any unstrung, meaningless existence, but to participation with God in bringing our society and ourselves into his Kingdom. The peace he offers is the assurance that underneath us are the everlasting arms.

Julia Ward Howe was in Washington when the Union Army suffered its disastrous rout at the Battle of Bull Run. She had believed passionately in the freedom of the Negro, and it seemed as if this was the end of her hope. From her hotel window she could see the camp fires of the Confederate Army. But later on she visited the troops, and then she wrote a poem that became one of the great hymns of the church. It begins:

> Mine eyes have seen the glory of the coming of the Lord;
> He is trampling out the vintage where the grapes of wrath are stored;
> He has loosed the fateful lightning of his terrible swift sword;
> His truth is marching on.

And so it is that this peace which our Lord offers us is rooted in our faith in God. It is the confidence of people who are engaged in the great struggle for a better world and a redeemed humanity. Let us not forget that Jesus said it was the kind of peace which the world could never give, but neither could the world take it away. This is what we are promised and this is what we may claim.

ᦟ 9 ᦞ

I Can Leap Over a Wall

Yea, by thee I can crush a troop;
and by my God I can leap over a wall.

PSALM 18:29

ONE OF the Old Testament books most used by Christians is the Books of Psalms. It deals with every emotion and it reflects every human mood. There are moments when the writer speaks words of faith and comfort, but there are other times when he expresses the agony of doubt and despair. There are psalms of joy and triumph and there are psalms of discouragement and fear. No matter how a man may be feeling, he is almost sure to find his mood reflected somewhere in this book. It is no wonder that we have published New Testaments which include the Book of Psalms. It is as if we were being told that if we should lose everything except one book in the Old Testament, we must never lose this ancient book of Hebrew poetry.

In the 18th Psalm we are confronted suddenly by words that sound as if they had been written by a teenager. There is exuberance in them and the sense of life so thrilling that he must shout it to the world. He is talking about the experience of God filling his heart, and he writes, "By my God I can leap over a wall." There is nothing that can bind me or hold me if I know the presence of God, is what he is saying. Life is unlimited and all things are possible if a man

knows God. It is a great word for our generation in a day when life
seems to close in on us.

Perhaps that is the first thing we ought to note—

Life Closes In.

There was a song we heard a good deal a few years ago with the
refrain "Don't fence me in." A psychologist analyzed its popularity
and concluded that every man feels fenced in and every man wants
to protest. Civilization has a way of surrounding people with limits
and obligations so that the free and natural life of the past appears
as utopia.

I am sure that this accounts for the popularity of western movies
or TV programs. We have had enough psychological dramas and
problem situations. The man who rides out across the plain is a free
man, or at least he seems so to us. Nothing is ever said about income
taxes or traffic rules, and the man in the saddle is the king of all he
surveys because he is free. Even evil is a relatively simple matter to
handle. If a man has a six-gun and is a good shot, he can solve all
the problems of society. The western reflects a kind of life we would
return to if we could, and for the city dweller, it is heaven.

Our physical life gradually runs down with the years. It comes
about imperceptibly, but there is a day when the most stubborn have
to admit they cannot run as fast or work as long without weariness.
The wear and tear of the years rob us of our resilience and stab us
with pain when we forget our age. Sometimes a disease attacks us
and we live under the handicap of ill health. Now our plans have to
be made within the confines of limitations of strength and we have
to plan tentatively.

The routine of living closes in on us. There was a man who
calculated how many times he would have to shave if he lived out
his normal expectancy. It so upset him that he decided he would
raise a beard. Well, you can imagine what happened to him! There
are so many things that have to be done every day whether we are
housewives, millionaires, or unemployed. There are so many things

never finished but repetitious and monotonous. It is the sheer boredom of doing the same thing over and over again that drives many a person to the edge of the precipice. We seem to be surrounded by tiring, nagging duties from which there is no escape.

Work closes in on us. Think of the man who has a tiresome job he hates but who knows that he is now doomed to do it five days a week until death or retirement. Even those of us who have interesting jobs which we would not trade with any other man, find they include large areas that are not inspirational at all. As the years go by, it sometimes seems that the interesting part grows smaller and the dull part grows larger. If we neglect the routine then we discover that the inspiration fades also. There is no escape. Every man's work is built upon the foundation of duties which are not inspiring. But they represent the necessary foundation without which nothing stands.

If life closes in on us physically, it has a tendency to do so spiritually. When did we last read a book? There was a time when our minds were attracted to hard, solid reading, and the greatest thrill that came to us was a new idea. For many of us those days are long since past, and we have fallen into the habit of skimming through the newspaper with most time spent on the comics. Once in a while we will get through a popular novel and now and again we will read a magazine article. There are exceptions, but in most cases we must confess that our reading has become sporadic and shallow.

Or we may consider our mental life and come to the same melancholy conclusion. We like cozy thoughts, small talk, bland conversation, and so we tend to move among the people who think as we think, whose ideas do not challenge us or contradict us. The burst of a startling new insight probably has not come to us for a long time. Gradually we have assumed that politically, economically, or morally everything has been decided for us and we are now simply keepers of the tradition. Indeed, we have difficulty in being the least bit tolerant of those whose positions threaten our right-thinking ways. When we meet a man whose thoughts are fresh, new, and adventurous, we are astounded because he is so unusual.

Is it not true that the same attitude is applied to our religion? I know nothing more distressing for the church than the number of its members who have not had a new idea about God in thirty years. The physical universe has expanded, but the God of that universe is still the childish one we adopted when we were twelve years old. If the experiences of life would broaden our vision of God, we would be better able to live in this enlarging universe. Religious boredom sets in only when religion ceases to be a broadening influence. The old-time religion may be good enough to sing about, but it is a stultifying influence unless it is leading us to say with increasing wonderment: "How great Thou art."

There was a simple German peasant who learned to read late in life. The thrilling adventure of his evenings was to pore over great writers of the past in an eager attempt to get acquainted with all of them. One day in a great burst of enthusiasm, he placed over his doorway: "Dante, Molière, and Shakespeare live here." There was a man for whom life had expanded even as the psalmist said it had happened to him.

Now it is also true that

Life Gets Blocked.

When we are young, this does not appear as a problem or even as a possibility. The problems youth faces are not obstacles in the way but too many wide open roads. Life is a matter of choice, and woe unto young people who cannot make up their minds. For in an amazingly short time the roads begin to get blocked off, and before he is aware of it, a young man knows that some opportunities are no longer options. It becomes increasingly difficult to get back to school after a certain age. By the time we reach thirty, some employers say they prefer people in their twenties. We may take some comfort when we arrive at forty in remembering a book that promised life begins at that age. Do not be misled and do not take this too seriously. Actually, doors have closed by that time and they are almost impossible to open. I remember that when I had the dubious honor of being the youngest bishop in the Church, one of my elder colleagues told me I would be surprised how soon this embarrassment would be removed. The period when everything is open is a very short one.

Failure blocks off the way. We have tried something and it did not work, which means we cannot go in that direction again. There are so many things that seem possible theoretically but are actually not possible. I am still amazed at the number of people who can spell out dreams and theories with great conviction in the face of what any practical man knows will not work. One of the lessons life teaches us early is the wide gap between hopes and realities. After a man has lived a few years and tried out some of his favorite plans, he knows that many roads are now closed.

Obligations block us off from the fulfillment of desires. Here is a man who would like to drop what he is doing and try something new, but he has a family depending on him for support. If he were alone he might try a new direction, but he dare not risk it with so many hostages given to fortune. Or he may have agreed to see a job through and he can only run away from it by denying a promise. To be a man is to be in relationships and that means responsibilities. There are times when we feel as if we were walled around with duties and demands.

Think of the number of people who have to settle for the second best and are prevented from realizing their first choice. I was having an annual physical checkup in a hospital one time when a young man came in to take a sample of my blood. He was a sharp, attractive youngster and I said I supposed he was going to be a doctor. No, he was not going to be a doctor, he told me, but he was going to be a technician. He said he had wanted to be a doctor but it had not worked out, and I did not ask him why. Perhaps it was because he lacked ability, although he looked very bright, or perhaps it was because of financial problems. But with what seemed to me a determined effort to look upon the best side of it, he told me that technicians played a very important part and that they made a good salary. I thought to myself that here was a young man who early in life was blocked from his first choice and must adjust to the second best.

Consider the people who dream of some large accomplishment and who come to a time when they know it will never be realized. They may have felt a great creative urge rising up within them, but it never quite came off. Perhaps it was more difficult than they thought. Perhaps it demanded gifts they did not have. The world is full of people who aimed high but who never hit the target. For them life has become a matter of adjusting to the second best.

We are likely to dream of a position that gives us status and position in society. People will admire us and look up to us because of the jobs we hold and the things we have accomplished. We want our names known beyond the small circle of our friends and we want to be listed in *Who's Who*. Sometimes it works that way and sometimes it does not. There are few people in the world who would not have to confess that their way has been blocked and they have had to settle for something that was not their first choice.

I saw a story in the newspaper about a man in Kentucky who had an amazing hound. He was a fast runner but he was a kind of pacifist. He never wanted to kill anything. He would come up behind a fox, put on an extra burst of speed, and run right on past him. The man said he had never seen so much frustration in all his life as when the fox suddenly discovered he was chasing the hound and couldn't keep up with him. People are sometimes like that hound and use all their energy to run fast, but they never capture anything. They might have achieved the goal at one time, but they ran right past it. Now it is too late to turn back. For one of the traps life lays for us is to assume that the running is an end in itself and whether we catch anything is unimportant.

For those who find life closing in or getting blocked off, there is good news. The psalmist says that

Walls Can Be Jumped Over.

No one can tell for sure what the psalmist meant, so let me suggest four things he might have had in mind.

There is a wall of *cynicism* and there are always plenty of reasons to feel cynical. A man does not have to look very hard to find illustrations of hypocrisy in high places. It is not difficult to discover that many things are not what they appear. Once we get suspicious we discover many reasons for our suspicion, and the cynicism which marks some men is a natural product of a point of view. It cannot be denied that the cynic has facts to bolster up his position.

The answer is surely not cultivation of a romantic outlook which can see only sweetness and light. Christians were never meant to be people blind to reality, and if Jesus told us to be innocent as doves, he also warned us to be as wise as serpents. The harm of cynicism is what it does to the cynic, and if there is any way for us to escape its enslavement, we need to hear it. Our Lord helps us to look at the worst and see beyond it to the best. It is a vision of something beyond tragedy which he shares with his followers. He brings to us faith that knows the worst but can believe the best. For when we see life steadily and whole, we are aware of goodness and greatness. We can condition ourselves to narrowness, bigotry, and meanness. He teaches us to go on to beauty, truth, and honor.

Dean William Inge of St. Paul's Cathedral, London, was sometimes referred to as "the gloomy dean." But he had a saving sense of humor, and noting the bitter and mean outlook of so many self-righteous persons, he said of them, "We who know them on earth can understand that their appearance in heaven will not be greeted with enthusiasm." Let us thank God that we can be saved from such bitterness and smallness which is the mark of the cynic and that God gives us power to leap over these walls.

Another wall the psalmist might have had in mind was *prejudice*. The prejudiced man lives in a small, selfish world which does not allow him to experience anything new or strange. While the barriers are raised within his own mind, this does not make them any the less real or confining. He is separated from the wider realms of humanity.

I doubt that any man is free completely from this disease of the mind and spirit. Now and again somebody will tell me I must understand he is not the least bit prejudiced. Usually this is prologue to the description of an attitude which appears to be naked prejudice to any neutral observer. But he is still clinging to the illusion that his attitude comes from his intelligence. I know I am prejudiced. The only safety is the realization that my mind works that way and to be on my guard. There are certain subjects I have the greatest difficulty in considering objectively. There are certain words which trigger my opposition and certain people who make me want to disagree no matter what they say. As a man grows older his prejudices tend to increase, and if he is not very careful, he will find himself walled in by them.

Some years ago Dr. Charles Drew developed a method of blood-plasma transfusion that has saved numberless lives. Many a man owes his life to this discovery and all of us are in debt to it. Dr. Drew was traveling in the South one time and became involved in an automobile accident which severed a large blood vessel. He was refused admittance at the nearest hospital because he was a Negro, and he died because he could not receive the help of his own medical discovery. If you are looking for an example of evil prejudice, here it is. It will be a great day when men can jump over that wall. Let us rejoice that Christian men are showing the way of escape.

Look at the wall of *hatred* and the way it crowds us into a small place. That men will always differ theologically is inevitable, and this difference need not be tragic in the least. Every fundamentalist is benefited by his liberal brother and every liberal Christian can profit from the conservative. I do not know anything more enlightening than to talk theology with somebody from a different camp. But if you meet a man who hates everybody differing from him, there is no profit in talking with him. I have dear friends who are more conservative than I am and I have some very fine friends who are more liberal than I am. Our differences do not need to separate us. But if we should hate one another, we would build walls between us.

In our time, the bitterness between economic and political liberals and the far right, has poisoned whole communities. If America cannot have an election without setting loose a spirit of hatred, our democracy is in danger. It seems to me quite obvious that we need liberal trends in our society and we need conservative convictions. But when these two things are separated by intolerant bitterness, society is sick. Believe me, we need help in leaping over these walls.

A friend of mine retired from a theological seminary faculty recently and I was reminded of our relationship through many years. His theology seems to me to be so extremely liberal that I have a hard time considering it with any sympathy at all. Sometimes in moments of extreme exasperation I have said to him: "Bill, how can such a nice fellow have such lousy theology?" He has always replied, "And how can a fellow smart enough to fool the Church and get elected a bishop be so reactionary?" How fine it is when God helps us leap the walls which might separate us and holds us together in the fellowship of Christ.

How shall we get over the wall of *fear?* I meet people who are frightened to death of the future, and they cling to what is familiar even when it is obviously outgrown. Tomorrow must always be worse than today, according to their judgment, and therefore they must prevent any change or any advance. Fear of tragedy drives us to the most ridiculous precautions and oftentimes prevents us from normal living. Fear of life itself surrounds many a man like a wall. It is good news then that God gives us faith to escape these fears which haunt us.

When Sir Francis Drake came to the Isthmus of Panama in the sixteenth century, he marched inland and climbed a tree. For the first time the wonder of the Pacific Ocean burst upon him and he cried out, "Almighty God, of thy goodness give me life and leave to sail once in an English ship on that sea!" So to the religious man there comes a vision of what life can be in its immensity and freedom. Like Sir Francis Drake he cries out to live it to the full without being walled in with cynicism, prejudice, hatred, and fear. God answers that prayer, and we rejoice with the psalmist that our imprisonment is ended and we can leap over the walls.

✃ IO ✄

Time for Decision

And those who went before and those who followed cried out, "Hosanna! Blessed is he who
comes in the name of the Lord!" MARK 11:9

PALM SUNDAY is one of the great Christian festivals, but I must
confess that it has always been somewhat of a puzzle to me. What is
the day supposed to signify? Is it simply a reminder that people who
shout hosanna on one day will be shouting crucify him a few days
later? Is it to celebrate the instability of men and the unreliability of
the crowd? It must mean something more than this or the Christian
Church would never have kept it as a central part of its liturgical
year for nearly two thousand years.

It came to me some time ago that this is a day reminding us of the
necessity for decision. It was the day Jesus made clear who he was
and proclaimed it publicly. Men had to accept him or deny him
now, and on their decision there rested the issues of life and death.

Joshua at the end of his career called all the people together and
said to them, "And if you be unwilling to serve the Lord, choose this
day whom you will serve, whether the gods your father served in
the region beyond the River, or the gods of the Amorites in whose
land you dwell; but as for me and my house, we will serve the
Lord" (24:15). The great leaders present these decisive moments to
the people and insist on a decision and a choice. The Bible is a book

of decision, and the God of the Bible confronts His people continually with the demand to choose this day.

We would eliminate this from our religion if we could. We hate to be put in a corner where we have to say yes or no. We much prefer a kind of faith that simply encourages us and quiets our fears. But the Gospel will have nothing to do with this approach, and it confronts us with the hard demand of either denying him and going our own way or accepting him as the Messiah and the Lord of our lives.

To begin with, let us consider

The Tragedy of Indecision.

I followed a man one time who was easily the most popular minister I ever knew. Nowhere did I find anyone with a harsh word to speak against him. He was universally beloved. Once in a while a man would say apologetically that my predecessor had a hard time making up his mind. But this was said lovingly and with no hint of criticism.

Yet I never followed a man who had made more of a mess of the church's work. The decisions which should have been made years before had been pushed off into a corner. Issues which needed to be settled for the good of the church had been ignored and neglected. Now it all descended upon me, for time had caught up with us. I remember thinking to myself that in the future I hoped my predecessor would be a man who might have made some mistakes but at least had made some decisions. Deliver me, O Lord, from a man who has won his popularity at the expense of personal responsibility.

This is an important word for the nation. Surely, it says something about us that we found it necessary to appoint a committee to determine our national goals. Does this mean that we have drifted for so long that we no longer know where we are going? It is a very easy thing for a nation to cover up a bad situation temporarily and go around it. But soon or late there bursts upon us a postponed crisis, only by now it has grown one hundred times worse. The statesman who is worth his salt will not win support by letting the people believe that they do not have to decide. Postponement is usually tragedy.

A corporation may fall into the trap of refining its methods of procedure and assume that it is keeping up-to-date. The president of the Carnegie Foundation one time remarked that it was easy for large businesses to come out with an enlarged edition of the rule book whenever there was a problem. Rather than decide upon matters which may be painful to us, we prefer to increase the regulations which never get to the heart of the problem.

How often the Church prefers rules to decisions. We can so easily become an institution with great traditions but no sense of mission. I have heard laymen bewail our present failure and talk about the good old days when mass evangelism made such a large splash in a community. How much better it would be if these churchmen would sit down without any nostalgia and find out what God is demanding of the Church in this particular moment. Too often we drift through the present crisis by reminiscing about a happier day. It is not that the Church does the wrong thing so much as that the Church so often does nothing. Bad men triumph because good men do not act.

So far as personal life is concerned, the disease of inaction can become so serious that we become neurotic. Psychologists tell us that sometimes people hover between different decisions in agony and finally remain in the middle, neutral, unable to decide. It is the old story of the donkey starving to death between two stacks of hay, unable to make up its mind which is the better. Shall I go to the theater or shall I call on a friend? So the debate goes back and forth, and a man finally ends up by staying at home, which would not be a bad idea if he had decided definitely to use his evening for something beside worrying. If the sickness gets bad enough, we have to go to a hospital, but most of us do not go quite that far. Yet the tragedy of our indecision shows itself in a worried life that produces amazingly little result.

How many men do we know whose work has been scattered and

dissipated by too many little interests and too much hesitation. If the fellow who has only one talent knows it and uses it with all his might, he comes out ahead of the man with ten talents who never learned concentration. A little of everything is a sad state of affairs and the disease of gifted men. Blessed is the man who has made up his mind what he wants to do and has accepted the discipline to turn his back on everything that does not put him on his way.

When Paul argued so eloquently before King Agrippa in prison, you recall that the king finally said, "Almost thou persuadest me to be a Christian." In that sentence there is the tragedy of many lives. Presented with great possibilities, they almost decide but not quite. Most of us looking back upon our life would have to say that there were moments when we came very near to doing a daring and wonderful thing. In my own experience I have hardly ever regretted decisions which were big and exciting, but I have nearly always regretted having turned my back upon them. There is no regret like the safe life that dwells in the twilight of mediocrity. For in spite of its triteness, it is true that it is better to have loved even when you lose, than to have been afraid to love at all.

A man was filling out an application for a job in a factory. He puzzled for some time over this question, "Person to notify in case of accident?" Finally he wrote down, "Anybody in sight." When there is a real crisis, never mind the fine points but go right to the heart of the problem. We do not always have time to debate, and the man who must always postpone will find that the events pass him by. There is a time for decision, and to do nothing is to fail.

Now another thing to say is that

Life Is Commitment.

Because the Gospel has to do with life it has to do with committing ourselves. The attitude that turns a man into a mere bystander has no encouragement from Christianity. Living is too serious a matter to be treated as anything less than a call for a full-time response on our part.

A man's life is a symbol at best, and no one can make much of a case for the ultimate value of a body inhabiting the earth for seventy years or so. When we begin to analyze the meaning of these years, it finally comes down to what we have stood for and what our years have symbolized. The trouble is that the physical things of life are so limited and so confined. He who makes his living a matter of physical experience only finds that after a few years, there is nothing much left and his life is a gradual running down. If we are to think of it in these terms, then the animal has it all over us and we are pitiful creatures who have been cheated.

But life is not only an intellectual matter either, and when we try to live it on this basis, we become less than human. To be in the presence of a thinking machine is to feel the cold blast of terror. Woe unto a man who has no emotional life and cannot weep or laugh. What kind of a life is it after all, that cannot express sympathy and concern? To deal with every subject from a purely intellectual standpoint is to make of humanity a horrible thing and completely unworthy of the Creator.

Now and again we meet a person who seems to have emphasized the spiritual part of his life to the exclusion of everything else. The result is not a happy one. Such persons dwell in an unreal world and despise the physical and social things. These are the people who are always going on retreats and seem to believe that to be religious means to meditate and think other-worldly thoughts. A man is a unity of body, mind, and spirit. No part can be split off and made supreme while ignoring the other parts. Life is a journey, but the experiences of the journey are a main value of life. It is true for men who must live that getting there is half the fun. We sing about that "land that is fairer than day" and look at it through the eyes of faith. But we are not there yet, and in the meantime we are to commit ourselves to living in the world God loved, and to the people who are His children and our brethren.

What we remember about a man is what he stood for and what he incarnated. Did he commit himself to causes which will be here after he is gone and to values which are more precious than life?

Woe unto the man who has found nothing greater to give his devotion to than his own welfare and his own pleasure.

The Bible witnesses to the greatness of human life and to its dignity. But strangely enough, it also insists that the dignity is to be realized only through service. Jesus said that if we would be great, we must become servants, and we discover one day this is the only way to become great. At about the same time the Aga Khan died, Amos Alonzo Stagg came to the end of his long life. A newspaper reporter pointed out the contrast between the two men and how cheap the wealthy ruler appeared who had pursued his own pleasure, compared to the old man whose life had been devoted to education.

Surely, our mistake is in choosing something to commit ourselves to which is not adequate. To serve our community is fine, but the man who can see no further than his community, lives in too small a world. To serve our nation is our duty and our privilege, but to be unable to see beyond national borders is to make life dangerous and limited. To be citizens of the whole world is a necessity of our time. But we discover one day that even when we confine ourselves to this world, we have taken too small an object for our devotion and our service.

It is the teaching of our Lord that until we feel under the orders of God, we are committed to something too small. Our faith teaches us that anything less than God is not enough, but that if a man commits himself to finding His will and doing it, his poor life will be enlarged. We can so easily miss the truth that to succeed in everything except in finding life full of meaning is to miss the essential. For as the psychiatrist, DuBois, one time remarked, "If a doctor can only see himself as a physical therapist, the only difference between him and a veterinarian is the clientele." The selfish materialist may believe he has chosen the right way because he centers his thoughts on his own welfare and comfort. But the truth is that the most miserable people in the world are those committed to themselves alone.

Now as we look back upon where we have come, we discover

The Big Moments Are Moments of Decision.

It was not just being good in the conventional sense or by conforming to what our neighbors seem to be satisfied with that has brought us a sense of having lived to the full. It has been, on the contrary, a time when we were confronted by One who challenged us to forget ourselves and follow him into some new venture.

In 480 b.c. the Persians were advancing into Europe and Leonidas with his small army of Greeks held them off at the Thermopylae Pass. Though he died in the attempt and nearly all of his men were killed, this was one of those decisive battles which saved Europe from Asian invasion. All that depended on that heroism could not have been known by the men who became the heroes. They simply committed themselves to their duty and to the defense of their people, and history made heroes of them.

In 1776 the Americans who took their courage in their hands and signed the Declaration of Independence had no guarantee of the future. Indeed, most people looking at it objectively would have said these were men doomed to die as traitors. For defeat would have sent them down through history as a group of well-meaning rebels who were executed. Commitment is not something with a guarantee attached to it, and the great moment is only seen to be great afterward.

William Booth, walking out of a Methodist Conference to do his work in his own way, was a man whose commitment was to something far beyond what his colleagues could vision. The story of the Salvation Army is familiar to most of us, but when the decision was made it looked anything but promising. He went out with his young wife, as he said later, without a friend or a farthing, but his sacrificial path led him straight to greatness.

When we look at our own lives and the decisions we have had to make, we know now that according to our faith, has it been unto us. How many boys facing their school had to make a decision as to how far they would go and how much education they would bargain for. I can remember a time when I realized that if I went on for graduate work and took a doctorate, certain commitments had to be made immediately. I can still recall the satisfaction when the commitments were made and I knew I had decided on extra time and more money than I could afford.

How significant is that moment of decision regarding marriage. If only we could see that this is not for a passing moment nor for a year but for a lifetime. I have known a number of young preachers whose lives were badly scarred because there was no common decision for the ministry when they chose a wife. Marriage is one of those decisive choices, and it is about as important as anything we do on this earth.

In our time we can choose jobs that will bring us a good income and give us security. If these are the primary elements in our choice, it will not be too difficult to make the decision. But suppose we have a sense of our work being our main contribution to the world and to the Kingdom of God? Suppose we decide that we want work that fulfills our best possibilities and demands everything we have? Suppose we want something much more than a legitimate racket where the money is plentiful? Then when we decide what we are going to do to earn a living, we are determining which way we shall go and what we shall become.

There is a sense in which character is primarily decisions. There is nothing that defines the quality of our lives as do those constant choices which harden into the habits upon which we build our future. I can remember yet walking around the block very much troubled before I finally registered at a theological seminary. I knew that this was a decisive time for me and that the bridges would be burned and the future defined once I became a theological student. But when it was done I gave a great sigh of relief and knew that God had called me and I was committed.

A man was walking along the beach when he heard a woman cry out for help. He looked up and saw a little boy being swept out into the ocean by a big wave. He had on a new suit and he was wearing a new watch, but he never hesitated a moment. He plunged in, swam to the boy, and brought him in safely. He looked down at his suit which was ruined and listened to his watch which had stopped. As the mother approached him he said in an embarrassed manner, "Oh, it was nothing, lady. It was nothing." And she replied, "What do you mean, it was nothing. Where is his hat?" Which is to say that a good decision does not always find its reward in appreciation from the outside. Its reward comes from the inner sense of joy at having committed oneself to something great and good. These are the moments of life which we never forget, for they are high points of human experience.

The last thing we ought to note is that

Christ Meets Us Today with His Demand for Decision.

There is a sense in which every day is Palm Sunday and we decide to hail him as the Messiah or wait for an easier and less demanding leader.

Our civilization today is face to face with the possibility of either greatness or destruction. The road taken will be decided not by the number of our hydrogen bombs but by the kind of men we have produced. The way we take and the great decisions we must make can lead us to life or to death. We stand again as did Israel, listening to somebody tell us that we must choose.

We must decide on our values and what we think is ultimate and essential. Our cleverness has led us to great material wealth. Whether or not we are at the end of something or at the beginning of something better will be decided by our commitment to our faith. The issues are clear enough, and it is no longer a matter of little practical significance whether we choose Christ. It has become literally for us a matter of life and death.

Studdert-Kennedy, who was a chaplain in World War I, wrote: "For God is love. Such is my faith, and such my reasons for it, and I find them strong enough. And you? You want to argue? Well, I can't. It is a choice. I choose Christ." He saw the essential nature of life. Sometimes we wish God would settle for half of our time and be content with a half day a week. But actually, there is no middle ground and the decision has to be all that we have. Jesus was no sentimentalist but a realist who was concerned that men fulfill their destiny as the sons of God. He comes with a complete demand for a complete decision.

Ring Lardner's "Big Time Story" tells of Mr. Big who is describing his impression of hotel life. He says, "Everybody puts on their evening clothes, like something was going to happen but it don't." That is the story of too many lives. Or perhaps it is better to put it in the fine words of Winston Churchill, describing the situation facing the Allies in 1943. He had said that if it was not the beginning of the end, at least it was the end of the beginning, and he wrote, "Between victory and survival there are many stages. Henceforth our danger was not destruction but stalemate." Is that not the danger of most lives? What a wonderful thing it is that Christ finds us and will not let us drift into a meaningless existence. With him it is a commitment and a decision which lead us to abundant life.

❧ II ❧

God in the Narrow Places

Then the angel of the Lord went ahead, and
stood in a narrow place, where there was no way
to turn either to the right or to the left.

Numbers 22:26

THE STORY of Balaam and his talking animal is a most intriguing one. Israel was camped on the plains of Moab near Jericho. The Moabites under their king, Balak, were afraid of this invasion and the king sent for a foreign prophet named Balaam to come and curse the Israelites before he fought against them. After entertaining the messengers for the night, Balaam started out the next morning to meet with the king of Moab. On the way the ass behaved very strangely, for it could see an angel of the Lord standing on the path, though the men present could not see him. Balaam struck the animal because it would not go forward and because it pressed up against the wall, bruising his foot. Finally, the animal lay down and refused to go forward, whereupon Balaam beat him and the Lord gave the ass the power to speak. Then Balaam's eyes were opened and he too saw the angel of the Lord standing in a narrow place where there was no way to turn either to the right or to the left.

How many times we find that in such a place is where God meets us. We seem boxed in on every side with no place for us to escape. It is in such moments of desperation that a man may receive the vision. For as it happened to Balaam centuries ago, so we may have our eyes opened to find that the angel of the Lord bars our way and speaks the word to save us.

Surely it is a general human tendency not to find the deepest experiences of our religion until we have to. Men do not become religious easily, but out of sheer necessity. It is the time when all human power fails and all human answers are inadequate that our eyes are opened to God. Let us think for a time concerning the God who meets us in the narrow places of our lives.

The first thing to note is that

We Try to Be Self-Sufficient.

The longing for independence and personal security drives us to all kinds of extremes rather than become dependent upon forces beyond our control.

Much of this is good. It is the story of growing up, and one of the delights of life is to watch children becoming more and more able to do things for themselves. We watch the baby grow until he stands on his own feet and walks. We watch our children turn to us for every need of life until the time when they begin to provide for themselves. The main purpose of living seems to be to achieve maturity. We watch this process in every generation with pleasure and some approbation. It would be a terrible thing indeed to have a child who had no desire to do things for himself.

We see young men and young women claim a new freedom and attain a new experience. Sometimes they do very foolish things, and they believe things which their elders know are not true. Still, we would not have it any other way, and this continuing story of growing from helplessness to sufficiency makes the human story always exciting and fresh. Young men like to repeat William Ernest Henley's words about being master of their fate and captain of their soul, which is mostly nonsense. But it would be a sad day indeed if they did not feel that great assurance that comes when for the first time they begin to make their own decisions and choose their own paths.

This is what we are seeing in our world today as the new nations are born. Without experience and responsibility some of these people are doing very unwise things and speaking some very unwise words. Let us understand it in terms of adolescence and have sympathy. Some of them are walking as free people in the midst of a very complicated world for the first time. After centuries of colonialism and subjugation, now they face the future with a new sense of freedom. It is a time for great patience on the part of the great powers, and the future is bright with the promise of these free people.

Besides the good results of this process, there are also some very bad ones. It is a source of much selfishness and hardheartedness. Life may have been kind to us and placed us in pleasant environments with natural resources at our disposal. We think that everybody else ought to win their own way and not count on outside help. We have been prosperous, so why should we worry about the poor and neglected parts of the earth? Let them do the same thing we have done and win their way as we have won ours. Of course, we forget that we may have been more fortunate than these people and that they suffer handicaps we never knew. An extreme doctrine of individualism can become a mean thing.

This pride in our own achievements sometimes puts us on the defensive, so that we cannot accept honest criticism. One week I had a blow because I read three things about parts of my Area which I resented. The first was a book called *The Green Felt Jungle* which intimated that the Las Vegas economy is gangster-ridden and under the control of disreputable characters. The Las Vegas Methodist Churches are under my supervision. I do not like to have such things said about one of my cities. In the second place, I read a book about Arizona that lampooned the "Cadillac Cowboys." Arizona is one of the most beautiful states in the Union, and I was upset to read how a man could satirize it. Then a magazine article talked about Los Angeles culture with tongue-in-cheek. That was really too much. I finally recovered, however, as I realized that nobody kicks a dead horse, and this country I love and call home is greater than any criticism anybody can hurl against it.

If we begin to take ourselves too seriously as we achieve independence, the usual result is ingratitude. We become ashamed to admit our dependence on other people. We forget the many times we have been helped by strangers. We seem to feel it is beneath us to admit our debts, and we want to play down everything that people did for us and play up everything we did for ourselves. Finally, we come to that ridiculous claim that we are self-made men. No man is self-made, and every man has been helped by friends and strangers to such an extent that his pride is destroyed if he is honest. But like Balaam of old, we tend to go our way and make our decisions without any attention to powers beyond ourselves.

One of the beautiful communities in California is Carmel, which has become an art center. It is a town with strict building regulations in order to maintain its beautiful atmosphere and appearance. Some time ago the mayor of Carmel was asked what his hopes were for the new year. He replied, "No new buildings in Carmel in the coming year . . . No improvements of any kind." He seemed to be saying that they were completely satisfied and they wanted nothing changed. But what he said is a reflection of what many a man has come to feel about himself. He thinks he is good enough and has done it all himself.

A second thing that needs to be said, however, is that

Life Is More than We Can Handle.

We are sufficient for a few of the simple things of life. But once one gets a vision of its mystery and wonder, he knows then that there are forces which by himself he shall never understand or control. The man who feels self-sufficient all his life lives in a mighty small world and adjusts himself to very small affairs.

The sense of our smallness comes to us sometimes in the presence of the big and splendid affairs of nature. Soon or late there is an experience which makes us feel as if all our human accomplishments are rather insignificant. There are very few of us who have not at one time or another felt a sense of great unknown mysteries which we do not understand and cannot even begin to describe.

Years ago when Admiral Byrd went to the South Pole and spent six months there by himself, he came back and wrote a book called *Alone*. Not many people would be able to stand the loneliness of days and nights of utter solitude. At one place in the book Byrd speaks of going outside his buried cabin and feeling the sense of a great rhythm of nature in the dying light of the sun. He felt the presence of something far beyond himself and a meaning which he could grasp only dimly. But it was there and for a moment he felt its reality.

What man can stand on the rim of the Grand Canyon and not have some sense of the forces at work which are overpowering? When we think of the millions of years involved in the carving of the Canyon and the beauty which has evolved from it, we begin to realize that man is a newcomer and in terms of the universe not so important as we usually think.

Or we catch a glimpse of the long sweep of history. We begin to have some sense of what Professor Loren Eisley called "The Immense Journey." Think of all the time involved in the development of man. How new we are and how inexperienced! Once we escape from the noisy events of today and take the long look, we stand in awe before this whole marvelous, mysterious process which has brought us to this day.

As each man looks into his own life, he is aware of what a mystery he is to himself. We are creatures who are beginning to penetrate the mysteries of the universe, but we do not understand our own souls. There are hidden impulses and possibilities which reveal themselves briefly here and there, but which seem to imply depths within us deeper than the ocean. How ridiculous it seems for anyone to assume that he can be self-sufficient in this kind of a universe.

We look at our country and we realize anew that there is the sign of a more than human power directing its growth and development. How did thirteen colonies ever develop into a nation like America? What has brought peoples from all over the world and molded them into a free society that has become the richest and most powerful nation of our time? How have we been saved from suicide and madness when we have endured the strange tactics of extremists in every generation? Where is the power of democracy and what is our hope for the future? I cannot escape the conclusion that America is a mystery and a dream, and in spite of all the dangers which threaten to undo it every year, there seems to be some unseen hidden force which preserves its life.

What a mystery is the Church! Always weak and always full of hypocrites, it is a fellowship with great aims though so full of contradictions. It is an organization but certainly different from anything else in the world. It has to deal with the very practical matters of drives and budgets, but its secret is not here. Its greatness lies in its faith and a consecration to an eternal Lord. There is nothing on the human side of the church's structure to make us believe that the gates of hell will not prevail against it. Only when we believe that the Holy Spirit of God is in it and uses it, do we have confidence in the long future of the Church.

Indeed, can any man believe he is self-sufficient? We have not been saved by our cleverness nor by our goodness but because of Someone who protects us and guides us. Life is too much for us, and the man who stands alone in his own foolish pride will come to despair soon or late. Self-sufficiency is the cry of the creature who is temporarily insane, and when the madness passes, he will learn soon enough that the power is not in himself. So we find ourselves in the strange position of seeking self-sufficiency and finally coming to the realization that we can never obtain it.

One day in the early part of 1964 I saw an unusual story in the *New York Herald Tribune*. The day before, New York City had held a civil service examination for horseshoers for the police department. Among the applicants was a twenty-three-year-old man who was raised in the Bronx. He did not seek the job with any sense of romance or because he came from a long line of blacksmiths. He confessed he was the victim of no education and it was his own fault. He had learned that education is important when it was too late. Then he said, "I might have been a lawyer, doctor, Indian chief, but I drive a truck in Brooklyn. And I don't like driving a truck. Too many nuts on the road. With horseshoeing, it's just me and the horse." My guess is that many a man feels the same way. Life gets to be too much for us, and if we could just retire to some quiet spot where the pressure would be less and the problems smaller, we would be delighted.

Now the third thing I want to say is that

Here Is Where God Meets Us.

How often the angel of the Lord waits for us until we come to that narrow place where we cannot turn to the left or the right. Usually that is the first time we can hear Him and that is the first place where we cannot run away.

One of the great mysteries and wonders of all history is Israel. It is still a scandal that such a small country could be so important to so many people for such a long time. Who were they and what did they do that they should so profoundly influence civilization? Who gave them the Book that has been for millions of people the Book of Life? What is there about the Jews that enabled them to see these things with clarity and preach them with conviction? The answer, it seems to me, is that they were people who for most of their history walked the narrow path where there was no way to turn either to the right or to the left. They were confronted by God with situations that were too much for them to deal with in their own power. Out of their suffering and disappointment they were made sensitive to the One who chose them to be the bearers of His Word and witnesses to His care and concern.

I remember D-Day in 1944 when we waited anxiously for news of the Allied invasion of fortress Europe. I was pastor in Lincoln, Nebraska, and we had the church open from morning until afternoon for people to come and worship. The husbands, the brothers, the sweethearts, storming the beaches of Normandy, were held up before God by wives and sisters and loved ones. For we were on the narrow path and there was no way we could turn to the right or the left. We knew in that hour that only God could bring us through, and we committed those we loved to Him. I shall not forget how in one place in the service we sang, "O God Our Help in Ages Past." That was a moment when many a person had all his illusions of his self-sufficiency destroyed and he stood naked before God in his weakness. No matter how long I live, I shall remember June 6, 1944, as that time when along with my people I knew the vanity of pretending to be anything but helpless before God.

I have had the privilege during the past few years of visiting churches behind the Iron Curtain. I worshiped with a Baptist congregation in Russia and felt again the power of the Spirit as these people prayed and sang their hymns. Caught in the midst of a hostile environment, they were hearing the voice of God in a narrow place. I preached one Sunday morning to a congregation in Prague and could almost feel the reaching out of the people for some word of truth and hope. That was no place for a commentary on current events but a time for a word of faith in God. I sat with a man in a hotel in Poland as we talked quietly about what it meant to be a Christian in a communist nation. As I listened to him I thought how wonderful it would be if people in America could have such an experience and learn the essential thing of the Christian faith, namely, God is our refuge and our strength.

How often this happens to us in our individual experiences. There is the alcoholic, for example, who finally has to strike bottom before he can be helped. When he can no longer pretend but must confess that something is now beyond his control, God meets him. It is in this moment on the narrow path with no place to turn that he sees the angel of the Lord.

During the depression I talked to more than one man who told me that he never found what life was all about until he had gone bankrupt and had to start over again. He had lived his life assuming that a good income and things which money could buy were essential. He could not imagine himself going on without his job and his savings. But when everything was gone and he had to start over again, there was a Presence which assured him of values that are not affected by depressions.

Sometimes it is a personal tragedy. John Bright's long dedication to the repeal of the corn laws in England began with the death of his wife. It was then that Cobden came to him and said that there were many homes in England where there was sorrow and hopelessness and that Bright should now join him in a dedication to make things better. Indeed, I have talked to a considerable number of men who have told me that life began for them in the midst of an impossible situation, and they found their way to sanity and joy when the utter hopelessness of their situation enabled them to hear a voice they had never heard before.

There was a janitor in a big city bank who was sweeping up the floor of the president's office after banking hours. A telephone rang and he answered it. The excited voice at the other end demanded, "I want to know what the Federal Reserve Bank discount is, what the prime-paper rate is, and if all this foreign travel is going to upset our currency." "Mister," replied the janitor, "I told you all I know about banking when I said hello." It is a wonderful thing that some people who know very little about the intricate affairs of this life have made one clear discovery which carries them through anything that life can do to them. They know power to live by, and they have found the presence of God when they must walk the narrow places. This is wisdom more significant than all the worldly knowledge about success.

The last thing to say is that we can be sure that in the future

We Need Not Fear the Narrow Places.

This is the good news that springs out of our weakness and finds us in our hours of trouble.

St. Paul learned this and wrote about it with convincing power. He talked about the impossibility of doing what was good even when he knew it was good. He described the despair of being a victim of principalities and powers. He talked about discovering the source of his strength and how through Jesus Christ there had come to him salvation by faith. His life became a constant pageant while from the outside it must have looked only drab and difficult.

It is a wonderful thing that when we know our weakness, we find our strength. This discovery does not create weaklings but men confident that life never takes them to a place where God is not. This is the birth of fortitude in a man's soul. It is a great moment in a man's life when he no longer has to pretend to be stronger than he knows he is. It is a great discovery when he finds that he does not have to pretend but can confess his own inadequacy in the knowledge that God holds him up and guides him through.

We shall find ourselves in Balaam's situation many times. There is no way to escape the road that leads us into the narrow places where there is no place to turn. But that is where the angel of the Lord is waiting for us to turn us back if we are on the wrong road and to show us the way through if we must press forward. Indeed, it is true that often the greatest religious experience comes from just such places.

Some time ago in a sports magazine a man wrote about the popular new underwater sport of skindiving. It had come to mean for him release from the frustrations of his life and he wrote, "I am drawn to the sea and the undersea because it literally puts me in contact with the whole world. The land is a disconnected thing; the sea is not." Something of this is the experience of men who find everything blocked off and then discover God. You are in touch with the unlimited and the eternal. That a man's life may have this power undergird him in his hour of need is one of his greatest discoveries. For this is the promise that the angel of the Lord will meet us in the narrow place, where there is no way to turn either to the right or to the left.

🐦 12 🐦

Sickness by the Pool

When Jesus saw him and knew that he had been
lying there a long time, he said to him, "Do you
want to be healed?" The sick man answered him,
"Sir, I have no man to put me into the pool when
the water is troubled, and while I am going another steps down before me."   JOHN 5:6–7

SOME TIME ago I stood where this scene is supposed to have taken
place. But it is all different now, with the pool in a courtyard. In
the days of Jesus it was an open public place near the Sheep Gate.
From time to time the water bubbled up, and this was thought to be
caused by some divine action. The people believed that if a sick
person could bathe in the pool immediately after this turbulence of
the water, he would be healed. So the sick gathered in large
numbers and five porches were built for their convenience. There
was a man there who had been sick for thirty-eight years, and he
had never been able to get healed but he still waited.

One day Jesus came along and asked this man, "Do you want to
be healed?" The sick man answered that he had no one to help him
and that someone always got into the pool ahead of him. Then Jesus
said to him, "Rise, take up your pallet, and walk." And the man was
healed.

There is a similarity between that situation and ours. We, too, are
sick and we look for some special healing or some special power to
make us whole again. How desperately we need one to come along
and restore us to health. Let us look at that story in the light of our
modern needs.

The first thing to notice is

The Belief in Magic.

They thought a troubling of the water would cure them, and you may say that we have gone far beyond such superstition. But do not be too sure that we are beyond magic in seeking answers to our problems.

Medicine is certainly one field where science has made great contributions, and our medical knowledge helps us perform miracles of healing. But in our attitudes toward medicine, there is a vast amount of searching for answers and expecting healings that are far from scientific. We have been promised drugs which will cure worry and restore confidence with no bad effects. When the tranquilizers were first announced, it looked as if the psychiatrist and the professional counselor would soon be out of business. A man could take a pill and suddenly feel at peace with himself and the world. Why would he ever need the help of a psychologist or a minister? But we have discovered that it is not so easy and not so simple. Some of these tranquilizers have proved to be habit-forming, and I have worked with more than one individual who found it almost impossible to break the pill habit and be free again. Besides that, we find that these drugs can only touch the surface and give us temporary relief. They do not actually resolve the conflict which caused the trouble in the first place.

Medicine is always a two-edged sword with both healing power and destructive force. A great doctor said one time that if he were told a medicine was perfectly harmless, he would know also that it was perfectly useless. The magic expectation that a cure for our worries and fears is about to be found, does not seem to be anywhere near fulfillment. We continue, however, to look for some prescription which will work miracles for us. Drugs apparently are wonderful, but they are also dangerous.

Turn to the problem of losing weight. So many Americans are anxious to find a way to reduce because we are too rich, we eat too much, and we get too fat. Some time ago a man wrote a book about calories not counting, the theory being that you could eat whatever you pleased and still lose weight. I saw a reference somewhere to an indictment issued against the publishers of that book for having promised things that could not be fulfilled. A few years ago somebody wrote a book about praying our weight away. That would be a good trick if we could do it. How eagerly we reach out for an answer to the problem of overweight which involves no discipline.

The hunger for strange and exotic religion which is often so observable in Southern California, springs out of this same desire for a new and easy answer. The old-time religion is too hard for us, and we want a mystical import from the East preached to us preferably by a man wearing a long white robe and sandals. It will be more convincing if he also needs a haircut. The plain, hard truths of the Gospel are not for us if we can find a pleasant way to give us success without half trying.

According to the movies and TV programs, the answer seems to be liquor. Do you not get a little weary of hearing people caught up in some strain or difficulty saying, "We need a drink." That seems to be the solution to every problem until, as Billy Graham one time predicted, when these people come to die, they will probably call for the bartender.

What we are after is happiness without character. We seek contentment without having to pay any price for it. We want adequacy without discipline. And if this is not putting us into the realm of magic, I do not know what else to call it.

Some time ago I was thinking about three great old men I know. One is Stanley Jones, who has been preaching the Gospel for many years and who always impresses me with the exuberance of his joyous faith. Another was Albert Schweitzer, whom I followed around for a couple of days a few years ago in Lambaréné. Whatever criticism may be raised against him and his work, be sure that here was a great man and no one could be in his presence very long without being aware of it. Then there is Bishop Herbert Welch, now beyond his one hundredth birthday, who in our Council of Bishops meetings never reminisces but always looks toward the future. Was there any magical answer for these men and did they obtain these qualities by taking a drug? No, and all who think that healing is to be found from this source are doomed like the man in the story to wait forever and never find what they seek.

A man consulted a psychiatrist about the best thing to do for his children. He expected to receive advice about their training, their schooling, and the cultural advantages he ought to give them. But the psychiatrist, who was a very wise man, said simply, "The best thing a father can do for his children is love their mother." Ah, this is something we forget. The child who lives in a home where love is real is blessed far beyond the child whose father can write him a big check. The healing we need is something magic cannot give.

A second thing for us to notice is that he thought the trouble was

The Fault of Other People.

Self-pity is ever with us and always self-defeating.

I suppose that most of us have envy in our hearts for some people. I remember when I was in high school, I went through a period of feeling very sorry for myself because I knew boys who had so many advantages I never had. They came from rich families who could give them what they wanted, and their futures were bright. My parents were poor and we lived in the wrong part of town. Surely, if I could make nothing out of my life, it was not my fault, and I thought it very unfair to be denied the help other boys received from their parents.

Or we say that the breaks have come to others and that luck has passed us by. I think there can be no doubt that at times a man has an advantage because he is in the right place at the right time. But I have concluded with the passing years that this never is a legitimate reason for success or failure. The breaks of life tend to even up, and if I lose one today, I may gain one tomorrow. The main thing is to believe that the man who depends on luck will come to a sad end.

Or we may say that some have influential friends. No doubt a man in a strong position can do something for a friend from time to time. Politicians who end up in prison knew important people. But no man can be held up very long by his friends, for soon or late he must produce and stand on his own feet.

If we can blame it on other people, we feel at ease because we are relieved of personal responsibility. What would America do if it were not for the communists? I do not take the communist threat lightly, for it represents as serious a challenge as we have faced in all our history. But I believe also that if suddenly we should wake up one morning and find that communism had disappeared from the earth, all would not be well with us. It is altogether too easy to blame all our failures on "those dirty communists" and spend our time investigating and attacking people rather than actually trying to solve our problems. Attacks on communism become a way out for the professional patriot who finds it easier than making personal sacrifices for this country.

In the church we find the same spirit of blaming everything that goes wrong on anything but ourselves. I grow very weary of listening to alibis as to why we are not doing a better job and why we have failed to be a real influence in our society. There can be no healing for us until we realize that the cause of our ineffectiveness is within us and the responsibility is at our own door. When the church begins to be aware of its opportunities and resources and puts less emphasis on its problems and its weakness, we shall be healed and begin to heal others.

One of the most amazing things about the Bible is the way the familiar can never grow trite if we read with our eyes open. I was thinking about that as I reread the story of the Prodigal Son. How many times have I read it? Hundreds? Thousands? It is one of the most familiar passages of Scripture I know. Yet this time as I read the story something found me that I had never really noticed. You will remember that when the young man had taken his inheritance and gone away into the far country, the time came when he was poor, hungry, and defeated. He was feeding swine, and that is about as low down as a Jew could get. Then he said that he would rise and go to his father and say to him, "Father, I have sinned against heaven and before you; I am no longer worthy to be called your son; treat me as one of your hired servants." Now, no modern boy would have said that. He would have said his trouble was his father's fault for being too strict or it was his mother's fault for making him go to church too much. Or if he sought a more scientific alibi, a psychologist would have told him that he was the victim of a sibling rivalry. What a shocker it is to hear a boy stand up and say, "I am to blame and the fault is my own." But do you suppose that this is the secret of the healing and the restoration? Is this perhaps the climax and the turning point of the story? Well, think about it and consider the possibility that there can be no salvation for us until we accept our own responsibility.

There was a young preacher with an attractive wife who liked new clothes. She spent too much and they were in debt. Finally they had a council and she agreed not to buy anything without first talking it over. Then she went to town and came back with a new dress, and the young preacher said to her, "But, my dear, you promised me." She replied, "I know I did, but the devil tempted me." He answered, "You should have said, 'Get thee behind me, Satan.'" "Oh," she said, "I did, and he whispered, 'It fits so beautifully in the back.'" There has to come a time when we will not blame it on Satan or anything else but accept our personal responsibility for our condition.

Another thing to note, and this is a rather shocking observation, is that a good many of us have

A Preference for Sickness.

The sick man had been there for thirty-eight years, which is really making a career out of your weakness. It was not too bad a life. His friends brought him there in the morning and came for him at night. The city had provided shade from the sun and protection from the rain. Here he met his cronies, and they talked together through the day. They watched other people going about their work and bearing their burdens, which is always a pleasant recreation. After these years in all honesty he was not very anxious for a change. Jesus' question, "Do you want to be healed?" was more than rhetorical.

We protest the evils we must endure, but actually we do not sincerely want them removed from us. The sickness of our society is war. Nobody wants war. I doubt that in any audience in the United States anybody would stand up and say that he really believes in war and would hate to have its possibility removed. We would not find anybody in the Soviet Union saying that, nor indeed in any place around the world. We are unanimous in our hatred of war, and we desire to be rid of it with strong conviction. But what about the things that go with war? What about the prosperity which grows out of our preparedness? What about all those industries which are tied up with defense projects? What happens when the government wants to close out a naval establishment or an air base? If we hate war, we love the things that war gives us. It would be a good thing for someone to ask us as Jesus asked that sick man, "Do you really want to be healed?"

Or there is the danger of inflation which can destroy our economic security. We have seen what it did in China and in Germany. We know it is a constant danger and hangs over our head with a threat of ruin. Nobody wants inflation, but we like the things that go with it. It is nice to buy property for $20,000 and sell it in two years for $35,000. There is always an exhilaration in riding a rising market, and there are men who know how to manipulate this trend so that they make fortunes. There may be some who are caught with fixed incomes and who find inflation a heavy burden. But the business community as a whole is not among them. Do we want to be healed? Well, not very much. Certainly, not right now.

Is there any person who wants lung cancer? What a foolish question! Ah, but we want something the surgeon-general has warned us may produce it. What a hard time we have had in even getting a warning put inconspicuously on cigarettes. For this is a multi-million dollar business which means jobs and prosperity for many people. The man caught in the habit will not break it, and while reading the warnings, he will hope that he is the exception.

Somebody told me that the new name for Forest Lawn Cemetery is Marlboro Country. Very funny! And very tragic that men and women will try to joke about disease rather than be healed of it. Is there not hypocrisy in making such a fuss about the spray on cranberries a few years ago and finding it so difficult to make any progress in the fight against cigarettes? Do we want to be healed?

There is always a certain amount of satisfaction in being relieved of responsibility. The invalid may develop a subtle psychology that takes delight in being free from burdens other men have to bear. I want to be excused from carrying the heavy loads and doing the hard labor. As long as I am waiting to be healed, I have a perfect reason for being excused. I should like to believe that I am different from other people. I am made of finer stuff and cannot be expected to do the hard things that some men find themselves obliged to do. If I am sick you may be sure that no one can criticize me for following an easier path.

Sometimes we want to believe that we are too spiritual for the hard things of life. There are religious people who take this unconscious attitude even as some talented artists assume they are to be excused from the ordinary rules of courtesy and morality. One of the most dangerous temptations we face is to embrace an illness as a way to escape life. Do we really want to be healed? Here is a first question we have to face, and until we are honest in answering it, nobody can do very much for us. We need a vision of how great life is when it is lived with full acceptance of its sorrows as well as its joys, its responsibility as well as its privilege.

When D. H. Lawrence died in the south of France in 1930, there was talk of building a memorial to him in his hometown of Eastwood, Nottinghamshire, England. The town council even set aside land for a civic center to bear the famous writer's name. During all these years nothing has been done, and a newspaper reporter visited the town some time ago to ask why. Different people made different excuses, until finally he found a local man who simply said to him, "Lawrence never liked this town very much and we never liked him." In a brief moment all the excuses and alibis were blown away and the stark truth stood out. There was no memorial because no one wanted to build one. We had better inquire into our situation and ask ourselves if the reason we are not healed is because we really prefer our sickness.

The story comes to its happy ending because of

The Healing.

Not all of the New Testament stories end happily, but this one did. When at last Jesus broke through the pretense of the man's mind and helped him see what he wanted and needed, he was healed.

Jesus said to him in effect that he must make an effort to stand up and stop waiting for an angel. I have seen that scene in my imagination many times, and I have observed it actually in my own ministry. Suddenly a man believes that Jesus Christ can give him what he needs and he accepts it and he stands up.

Oftentimes the hardest thing in life is making the start. How long we can postpone the decision and the action! We are going to break a habit, but not until tomorrow. We are going to start our book, but not until a more convenient season. We are going to lift ourselves to a higher level, but not now. Then there are times when the miracle occurs and he says to us, "Stand up." Getting started is the hardest part, and if we can take him at his word and simply believe that now is the moment, we are healed. The great surprise that comes is the realization that joy is his gift to those who carry their share of the load. C. S. Lewis wrote an autobiography which he entitled *Surprised by Joy*. It is a fine insight that to take Jesus at his word is to find ourselves surprised by his joy.

According to our faith shall it be done unto us. According to our faith shall we find power. What a great thing it is to know that the Great Physician is as available to each one of us now as he was to that man by the pool.

There was a missionary in India who asked a Hindu scholar to teach him the language. The man refused. The missionary said he did not expect the service without cost and that he would pay the fee expected. But the Hindu still refused, saying that he did not want to become a Christian. The missionary promised to make no effort to convert him. All he wanted was to learn the language. Then the Hindu scholar replied, "No man could be with you very long without becoming a Christian." This is the way it ought to be and so seldom is. But the good news is that no man can walk with Jesus or accept his way without being made well. He will destroy our illusions, but he will give us health. And that, my dear brethren, is good news indeed.

❦ 13 ❧

Go Up, Take Possession

Behold, the Lord your God has set the land before you; go up, take possession, as the Lord, the
God of your fathers, has told you; do not fear or
be dismayed."   DEUTERONOMY 1:21

ONE OF the greatest of the books of the whole Bible is the Book of
Deuteronomy. It is quoted by all except six books of the New
Testament, and as it describes one of the great dramatic moments in
the history of Israel, it makes real the Word of God. In 621 B.C. King
Josiah instituted a great reform of Israel's life and worship. Most
scholars believe the reform was inspired by the finding of the Book
of Deuteronomy, or at least part of it, while the Temple was being
repaired. Some of the profound central insights of our faith are
announced, and here is proclaimed the greatness of God and Israel's
obligation to Him. The book consists of three addresses by Moses
which describe the acts of God, the law of God, and the covenant
with God. Deuteronomy is one of the high points of the Bible.

The book describes a crucial situation. The early conquests having
been accomplished, Israel now waits before the promised land. The
danger now is to settle down and adopt the customs and religion of
their neighbors. A generation has been spent in the Wilderness, and
here they are at the moment of decision. What next? Will they stop,
or will they go on and claim the land? Moses proclaims that God
has set the land before them and now they must go up and possess
it. It is a dramatic, decisive moment in the life of the people, and it
is the kind of situation which men and societies face sooner or later.

Let us begin by observing that in every man's life

There Is a Land To Be Possessed.

We may stop before actually winning it and content ourselves with a compromise. But God puts before men and societies a vision of places they ought to be, and lives they ought to live.

In our time the promised land is world peace, and we have made some advance in that direction. We now linger beyond the Jordan, and the hardest part of the fight probably is ahead of us. Many look upon the attainment of peace as impractical and impossible, but it seems obvious to me that God wills the nations to live in amity, and we must now gird ourselves for the final assault. We know it is there and we must proclaim that it is time to go up and possess it. There are a good many technical problems involved, no doubt, but the main thing is the will to do it and the vision to see it. This is the responsibility of the followers of the Prince of Peace, and for the first time in all history, the possession of this land is before us.

In America we have spoken bravely about freedom and liberty for many years. We have accomplished much, and this country has been a refuge for the oppressed and the enslaved. Yet, so far as entering the promised land itself, we have hovered on the outskirts and postponed the final assault. Today we are caught up in the midst of that last invasion, and there are many people who are unhappy. But think what it will mean if every American citizen is first class and every American child has equal opportunity. This is a great day for us because our Negro brethren are urging us to go up and possess the land.

The Church has been divided and too content to accept established patterns of organization. Now a fresh breeze is blowing and the mists are disappearing, leaving the land sharp and clear ahead. The old divisions are crumbling and we are speaking more in appreciation of one another and beginning to demonstrate more clearly that Christians ought to love one another. It is great to be living in a time when the voice of God comes to us through events and men to tell us it is time to move forward ecumenically.

In our personal experiences we face such moments and are

confronted by such decisions. Nothing is more confining than the selfish life, and there comes a moment when the inner voice commands us to enlarge our vision and expand our service. Truly at the end of the day a life that has contributed nothing to the common good is the great failure. Every man is commanded to go out beyond himself and claim a place in the healing ministry of the world.

It is a strange thing that our affluent society can produce so many comfortable lives that are so unhappy. I talked with a man not long ago who objected to the idea that there was anything very wrong with us. He pointed out all the advances in comfort we have made and all the social progress of the last fifty years. What he said was true, of course, but how do you explain the terrible fear in the hearts of so many people? What causes our anxiety and why is inner peace so hard to come by?

There is in each man's life some purpose which may have been a growing realization or a sudden discovery. But there it is, and once it has been recognized, there is no peace for him until he moves forward toward its accomplishment. Once Moses had reminded the people of who they were and what God had promised them, they could never be content on the other side of the Jordan. Nor can we. Call it a restless discontent or give it any naturalistic term you choose. The religious man knows it is God probing his heart and commanding him to go and possess that better place.

Some time ago John Crosby, a columnist for the *New York Herald Tribune,* asked, "Why is it that the most adventurous new buildings are all churches?" Coming from Mr. Crosby, this is a significant question. I was not aware that this is true, but I hope it is. The Church ought to be a symbol in its architecture and a promise in its life of spiritual adventure and moral progress. For the Church should point the way for societies and persons to a land of promise which ought to be and can be possessed.

But another thing we must note is that

The Wilderness Has a Great Attraction.

What we call civilization is forever under the attack of people who prefer the jungle. There is an ease and relaxation connected with the simple life of the savage which pulls civilized men in that direction. Always we stand in danger of slipping back to a lower level of life by people who are savages in their hearts. So we stand on the outskirts of the promised land, deciding whether to go forward and possess it or slip back quietly into the less demanding life of the wilderness.

Contemporary literature illustrates this attraction. The novel that revels in anatomical descriptions of the sex act implies that men will be happier if they no longer seek to control their sexual impulses. The naturalistic school of writing tries to make all restraint hypocritical and artificial. Such writers hold up doing what comes naturally as a sign of maturity.

We have been through such periods and probably there will be more of them in the future. New writers appear who seem to be vital and vigorous. But look at them objectively and they are simply extolling adolescent thought and behavior which we should have outgrown. Repression can be evil, but not always. Repression oftentimes makes the difference between a human being and an animal. The undisciplined life has its attraction, and always there are people who preach this gospel as if it were a new discovery and the promise of a new life. Actually, it is nothing of the kind. It is little more than the expression of a nostalgia for the wilderness.

When it comes to art I cannot speak with any authority at all. In this field I am ignorant and entirely a Philistine. Yet, when I look at some of the abstractions which seem to me no more than an arrangement of geometrical lines or the placing of blobs of color at will, I cannot think that they point to the future. What is despised as traditional also demands more skill and more discipline. The kind of painting which can be hung upside down in a museum for months without anybody noticing the difference seems to me symbolic of the wilderness and not the promised land.

The theater reflects that same situation. It is all right to have a stage setting that is merely suggestive, but as a great director one time pointed out in an honest moment, it is also easier. In the name of realism we are sometimes willing to wipe out all progress toward a better life and move backward toward the primitive. An excessive superficiality is not to be desired by any means, but let us not be misled by the urge to remove all restraint. The trouble with much modern drama is not that it is shocking—would that it were at least that! It is just dull and boring, and we ought to complain to the Better Business Bureau for taking our money under false pretenses.

When we turn to morals, we are told we must not be cabined and confined. In the name of freedom (really license) we are encouraged to seek paths that lead to indecency, as if this is new and progressive. I have, for example, been reading some things about the new topless bathing suits, and I have heard that there are some restaurants where the waitresses wear such costumes. This is progress? A few years ago in Africa I drove through the Congo with a young missionary. We saw lots of topless bathing suits all along the road and in every village where we stopped. Do we wish to return to that, or is there a difference between the way women dress in a civilized nation? You will forgive this allusion, but a leading fashion designer one time remarked that the most boring place in the world is a nudist camp. If we want to be rather nasty little boys out behind the barn, let us recognize the impulse for what it is. Actually, it is the call of the wilderness.

Each man has to decide whether he will pay the price for moving on or take the easier bargain and slip backward. License has its appeal without question, and if I could believe that this is the road to the future, how pleasant it would be. My only safety is to realize that such a way leads back from whence I have come. The disciplined road, while hard, offers rewards far beyond anything the jungle trail can produce.

All of us to some extent at least are lazy and we prefer ease to effort. I want the way that does not make too many demands on me. To go forward and upward means to say good-by to much animal comfort. But life consists of something more than the physical, and I must not be fooled by the wilderness call. The uninhibited person who is so often portrayed by our contemporaries as admirable, is very often nothing more than an utterly selfish individual who simply wants to do what he feels like doing. The man who takes social responsibility has admitted and accepted the claims of his brethren. Individualists make interesting biographies, but they are usually a danger and a snare. We shall be wise to learn as early as we can that doing just as we please is another name for savagery. As the Children of Israel paused before the promised land, so we stand often in the valley of decision. We need a Moses to tell us to go up and possess.

A man tells of having breakfast at the Kennedy International Airport in New York. A poorly dressed, desperate looking Cuban came in, waving a beer bottle. He began to speak in broken English about the situation in Cuba and insisted that America must pay more attention to it. He finally became a nuisance and the waitress said to him, "This is a business establishment. We don't want no trouble. Now get out!" The man was crestfallen but immediately left the restaurant. The diners all returned to their breakfast except an American sailor, who sat staring at his coffee. Suddenly he looked up and said to the waitress, "Look, he wasn't trying to make you no trouble. He was trying to tell you that you got trouble." Whenever a Moses comes along and commands us to go up and possess the land, he is not trying to cause us trouble. He is trying to tell us that if we do not escape the attraction of the wilderness, we have trouble.

For another thing, notice that

Here Is the Perennial Struggle Between Doubt and Faith.

Most of our life is lived on this battlefield. We live by faith, and the important decisions are either for the promised land or the wilderness.

If history teaches us anything with any clarity it is that the dangerous time for a people is the period of ease and prosperity. How sharply the Bible draws this lesson and how strange it is that the biblical writers seem to be less afraid of adversity than they are of success. Americans are not threatened by invasion today in spite of the hysteria of extremist groups. But we are in real danger of self-betrayal and self-destruction. Democracy wearies us, for it is difficult and demanding. How much easier it is to accept dictators and drop the burden of responsibility. Our faith in freedom is the deciding factor, and one of the evil things in our nation today is the Apostles of Discord sowing doubt in the name of patriotism.

Political parties live by their faith and not by their doubts. Once their leadership sees the promised land back toward the wilderness, their days are numbered. For men know deep inside that doubt has no future and they can only be saved by faith.

How easy it is for the Church to surrender its faith. How easy it is for us to settle for too little. How easy it is to adjust to the present condition and not keep the tension on our way of life. The Church is to proclaim and demonstrate faith, and it must never allow men to confuse comfort with progress. There is a sense in which the Christian Church must always stand before the people as Moses did, saying to them, "Behold, the Lord your God has set the land before you; go up, take possession, as the Lord, the God of your fathers, has told you; do not fear or be dismayed" (Deut. 1:21).

The tragedy of most lives is to settle for too little and be ruled by our doubts. Kierkegaard wrote one time, "When I read the New Testament I get the impression that in God's opinion every man is a giant. . . . How ironical that every man is designed to be an Atlas, capable of bearing the weight of the world—and then see what men we are; and alas, how sorry a thing it is that we ourselves are to blame for what we are." We adjust ourselves to our weakness rather than trust our strength.

When Alaska experienced a terrible earthquake a few years ago, the Governor's wife said that many phone calls came to the Governor's Mansion. She answered most of them, and usually they were demands that she do something for some relative or some friend. But she received a letter from a ten-year-old boy in the Midwest who sent her two nickels. "If you need any more," he wrote, "please let me know." There is faith in all its shining splendor! Two nickels are not much, but they were probably all the boy had. He was one of those persons who thought it was better to do his best even if it was small. This is faith, and it has power to overcome all the forces of doubt. For once it is observed in action, it lifts up the hearts of all the people who see it. Said Moses, "Behold, the Lord your God has set the land before you." The command is from God, and our response must trust His promise.

The final thing for us to observe is that

God's Command Carries with It the Promise of God's Help.

This is the wonderful thing about the demands He puts upon us. The New Testament says that we are never tempted beyond our powers to resist. It is my faith that God knows me better than I know myself, and He never gives me a burden I cannot bear. When it seems we cannot do what we ought to do, we have forgotten the power and support that come from Him.

How much we need the enthusiasm of a living faith in God. In the eighteenth century, religion had everything except power and enthusiasm. It sat on the edge of great new possibilities and did not move. It had cathedrals and clergymen, but the people felt no command to possess the land. Then John Wesley came along and got excited about what God had done for him and what he saw God doing for plain folks. A new spirit possessed him, and nothing was added except an experience of faith. Some churchmen were suspicious of these "enthusiasts," even as today. But when a man understands the resources which are promised him, it is hard not to shout with joy.

Today we are tempted to camp on the border of territories we should possess. We are the victims of fear that in an impersonal world, one man's witness does not count. But if we believe that God wills our invasion of these territories for Christ, what a wonderful moment it is. The conversion experience is usually a vision of new possibilities and a conviction that if we can see it, we can possess it.

We need renewal and the church needs it. How wearisome life can become when we bog down in routine. How monotonous existence can be and oftentimes is for men. But the Bible is always bringing us back to a great new vision of God and we are lifted up. For every man who lives on the edge of sadness and finds the future just more of the present weariness, there is good news. There is a better life than we have realized and there is a greater accomplishment than we have dared to expect. God is not through with us by any means, and it could be that even in this very hour, He plans to go with us into the promised land.

Christopher Morley, one day while observing the telephone, began to think of the people who were waiting somewhere to hear some good news. There were the parents waiting anxiously for a call from a boy or a girl far from home. There was the lonely young man in the city wishing that someone would call him and talk to him. There was the girl who was waiting for the young man to announce he was coming to take her to dinner. And he says that suddenly he wished he could call them all and give some good news to each. Well, this is what I have been commissioned to do. To every man, to every woman, to every young person who is dissatisfied, my word is that God wants you to possess a better life than you have ever known, and best of all, He will help you possess it.

ᦁ 14 ᦂ

One True Sentence

In the beginning was the Word. . . . And the
Word became flesh and dwelt among us. . . ."
JOHN 1:1 14

ERNEST HEMINGWAY's *A Moveable Feast* was published in 1964.
Hemingway had died in 1961, and the book is an earlier writing
describing his beginning days in Paris. While it had some bad
reviews, I found it easier to read and more rewarding than some of
his novels. He says in one place, "Sometimes when I was starting a
new story and I could not get it going, I would sit in front of the
fire and squeeze the peel of little oranges over the flames and watch
the sputter of blue that they made. I would stand and look out over
the roofs of Paris and think, 'Do not worry. You have always
written before and you will write now. All you have to do is write
one true sentence. Write the truest sentence that you know.' So
finally I would write one true sentence that I knew or had seen or
had heard someone say. If I started to write elaborately, or like
someone introducing or presenting something, I found that I could
cut that scrollwork or ornament out and throw it away and start
with the first true simple declarative sentence I had written."
Anyone who has ever tried to write or do any creative work knows
desperate moments when you are ready to begin but have nothing to
say. Hemingway discovered that a simple true sentence would get
him started when he was in that mood.

There came to my mind at once the Prologue of the Fourth Gospel. John is talking about a Word that was from the beginning and became flesh in Jesus Christ. Do you suppose he was saying something similar to the novelist? Is it true that God has given us one true word to get us going when we are rundown and hopeless? Is this how the Word saves us? Perhaps God works this way through Christ, and when we have come to the end of our courage and our purpose fades, it is the true Word that gives us new strength and vision. Let us consider this for a little while.

I should like to begin by looking at

The Way Men Go Wrong.

Young people usually think this is a rather simple problem and it has simple answers. They believe that a man goes wrong by simply betraying the right. It is as simple as a traitor selling his country, and the man who ends up a rascal is simply a Benedict Arnold who chose evil over goodness. Somewhere along the way, such an attitude suggests there was a dramatic moment when a man deliberately betrayed his own best self.

Or it may be that we see life as a road that divides. One fork is labeled right and the other is marked wrong. In a decisive moment when we turn on the one that leads to sin, our choice is clear-cut and definite. There is thought to be a particular moment when the wrong turning is taken deliberately.

We think that men get tired of well doing and in their weariness they switch their allegiance. They have borne the burden for a long time and suddenly they decide it is no longer worth bearing. They look for an easement of the struggle and they simply leave the battle and surrender. But in any case, the choice seems open, definite, and precise.

As we grow older we become aware that all of this is quite wrong. We seldom make decisions which are obvious and clear-cut. Two men were indicted for having stolen funds from their company. They were brought to trial and found guilty. As they were being taken away to begin long prison terms, one turned to the other and said, "John, what happened to us? We were decent boys and we were honorable young men. What has happened to us?" And that is the way it actually happens. There was no clear dramatic moment when the choice was made. There was no particular instance when those men could have said that they had made their decision to become thieves.

Some of the pictures of the Bible are not as meaningful to us as they were to an agricultural society. There is a sense in which we are in constant need of "de-mythologizing" the Scriptures. One of the pictures used in both the Old and New Testaments is the shepherd and his flock. The meaning of that illustration is not very clear to most of us urban dwellers who only now and again may see a flock of sheep along a country road. We have not the foggiest notion, so far as actual experience is concerned, of the nature of the relationship between sheep and shepherd. We do not know the characteristics of sheep. I read something some time ago that gave me a new understanding of the situation. The writer said that sheep "nibbled themselves lost." He said a sheep is drawn by a clump of grass and then another one, and he keeps on following the grass without looking up and never knows how far he has strayed from the flock. Finally, when he does look around, he discovers himself in a canyon far away from the shepherd and with the night coming on. He is lost, but as to the particular moment it happened, he has no idea. This is one way people resemble sheep, and this is the way we drift away into danger.

We get lost because we want to make our life easier. I heard a sermon many years ago by an American preacher on the subject: "How To Make Life Easier." I said to myself that people do not need much advice on that subject, for it is what we are always trying to do. Why should we live up to a high standard when nobody else is living up to it? Why should we submit to the discipline of high endeavor when we could be content with less discipline and less accomplished? Why must we be under the constant testing of being better than we want to be? Why not adjust ourselves to what is reasonable and stop straining for such high achievement?

We decide we will settle for the second-rate instead of the best. We decide we will take our place among the mediocre and be content with the average. The teaching of the New Testament begins to sound too difficult and too demanding. Imperceptibly we grow accustomed to the ordinary and we gradually adjust to the cheap.

We see this happen in so many ways to so many people. The playwright begins to trade on his reputation instead of on the quality of his next production. The book reviewer reads a book which is a little better than the one he read last week, and proclaims it to be a fine book. Actually, it may be a very poor one because his comparison lacks the long look and he has forgotten what a book ought to be. There is no true sentence and no true word which he looks at before making his judgment.

Men need some standard which haunts them and never lets them feel satisfied. Alfred North Whitehead, the American philosopher, said that we must have "the habitual vision of greatness." Hemingway said he needed one true sentence. The Fourth Gospel talks about the Word from God that came into the world and became flesh.

Now the other side of the coin is that we are safe only when we are under the judgment of the best. There is always need of a moral standard in society. I am not one to even hint that everything was all right in the good old days and everything is wrong with us. I do have a great fear that there is a gradual lowering of our moral levels simply because we have so few examples of proper moral aims. The rise of juvenile delinquency and the increasing divorce rate proclaim the need for one true word to make us aware of what life ought to be. Is there not a growing tendency among us to take our behavior patterns from the movies, from TV, and from novels? There is a tendency to take what the majority are doing as the norm.

We see the same leveling process in government when men betray their public trusts to become rich. A society which measures everything by the question of whether or not it contributes to prosperity finds it difficult to be shocked by public servants who are for sale. Whatever else may have happened to Rome, it seems quite clear that

the betrayal of trust by public administrators was one of the main
reasons for its decline. When the patrician felt he had no duty to
serve on the frontier but could pay someone else to do it while he
enjoyed the luxury of Rome, that was the beginning of the end. In
contrast to that, think of the American tradition which began at the
Constitutional Convention. When fifty-five men met to draw up the
American Constitution, they were not suddenly blessed with even
tempers and idealistic outlooks. They quarreled and some of the
debates were bitter. There came a time when the presiding officer,
George Washington, stood and said, "Let us raise a standard to
which the wise and the honest may repair. The event is in the hand
of God." It was that kind of word which saved the convention, and
it has been that kind of spirit through the years which has given us
government to be trusted and government leaders who put patriotism above profit.

I am sure we have a good many businessmen whose ethics are not
of the best. I am sure also that the businessmen of America have
been for the most part honorable and reputable. I remember a
meeting of a committee which was debating whether or not one of
our church institutions had to live up to a spoken promise given to
the County Board of Supervisors a few years previously. A legal
mind on the committee said there was no need to worry, since the
promise was not in writing. I remember, however, that a business-
man present said business was not conducted on that basis. He said
we had to determine what the understanding was and live up to it.
Is this as common a business attitude today as it once was?

What can we do so far as our personal life is concerned? What
can a father give to his son? What can a mother give to her
daughter? What is the home supposed to provide for the children?
The best thing is always an example of character, of ethical
behavior, of honesty which haunts the minds of children for as long
as they live. This is the priceless gift of a Christian home.

What does a teacher give students? I find myself forever in debt
to a few great teachers—more than I deserved. Most of the facts they
taught me, I have forgotten and now have to look them up in a

reference book. Some of the facts they taught me were not facts a few years later. But great teachers teach a love of truth and a respect for facts. They encourage a critical attitude and a desire to find reality. Such a spirit influences young life and gives it a pattern.

The task of the preacher is to hold the true Word before the congregation. If I were a layman and my preacher spoke to my likes every week, I would certainly request a change. The layman has a right to expect that the preacher will offend him from time to time, and now and again, the preacher ought to make him angry. By no means should he ever have to put up with a gentle voice speaking to his prejudices week after week. That kind of preaching brings death. As preachers we have the responsibility to call the attention of our people to another kingdom and a higher life. Every Sunday morning people ought to hear a true sentence spoken which will start them on the road upward for another week.

Now we come to the moment when we proclaim the Good News, which is that God has done all of this for us in Jesus Christ. Let me bear witness to St. John's affirmation that

Jesus Is the True Word.

The Incarnation is a mystery and beyond our understanding. But it is clear that in the life and teaching of our Lord, we have God's Word for us. It is amazing to note how the presence of Jesus Christ in the world brings us back to the straight path when we go astray and points the way to life. The English scholar, T. R. Glover, one time said, "Four words destroyed slavery, *'for whom Christ died.'* " This is something that many people have not understood. The very presence of Christ brings judgment upon nations, and the great reforms have come about because men could not be at ease with sinful compromise in his presence.

He is the true word about *God*. This is where we must always begin. Much of our modern difficulty springs from an assumption that we can solve other problems before we come to terms with God. In spite of our many accomplishments and our unquestionable cleverness, we are lost and grope for meaning until we have some clear word about God. H. G. Wells said this many years ago in his novel *Mr. Britling Sees It Through*. He said that God was the first and the last thing and that until a man finds God and is found by God, he begins at no beginning and he works to no end. This is a word we need to hear and heed.

Yet how shall a human mind comprehend the Lord of the universe? Our little minds cannot even imagine the distances He has created and the expanse of the universe. "Canst thou by searching find out God?" asks Job. The greatest minds of all time faltered when they tried to make clear to men the nature of God.

But in Jesus Christ we find enough knowledge of Him to live by. We have enough light shed upon His nature when we learn that God was in Christ reconciling the world to Himself. I may not be able to reason with the philosophers, but when I come into the presence of Jesus I know about the love of God and I glimpse something of divine purposes. In the midst of all the confusion of living this is the true sentence that starts me on my way.

Jesus Christ is the word about *life*. While we talk about it glibly our actions betray the sad fact that we do not believe in the sacredness of life. We are forever in danger of taking the cheap attitude toward others and toward ourselves. The history of human warfare is ample testimony of our hypocrisy, and in World War II we made no further pretense of marking a distinction between combatants and noncombatants. The whole process led us to an ultimate horror when we killed not only the enemy but his women and his children. Or if we look closer home, we see that we kill and maim about fifty thousand people a year on the highways of America. How seriously do we regard life when we allow the automobile to operate like a scourge across the land, especially over holidays? Or how sacred is life as portrayed by TV commercials? No wonder the cheap and the tawdry sweep away our discrimination and judgment.

No man understands his life any more than a medieval poet who said it was like a bird coming in from the darkness, flying across a lighted room, and then flying out on the other side into the darkness. From whence have we come and whither do we go? I am in need of a standard to keep me mindful of what my life is.

This is what Jesus Christ has been doing for men now for two thousand years. He is the one who rescued us from regarding some of our brethren as inferior. What a wonderful thing it is that his solitary life in Palestine speaks to modern men of their nature, their destiny, and their purposes. In the midst of the confusion of conflicting directions and contradicting philosophies, God has given us the Word about who we are and what we ought to be.

Will Rogers told about a druggist who was so tied up with his own business that he worked long hours and oftentimes seven days a week. Somebody asked him if he never took time off to have a good time. The druggist replied no, he did not, but he sold a lot of headache medicine to people who did. A generation that spends so much of its time trying to find a way to have a good time, can only be saved when it hears a saving word about what life is. That, my brethren, is the good news of the Gospel.

Finally let it be said that God has given us a true word about *man*. Are we animals? Yes, we are and our bodies bear testimony to our animal heritage. It is perfectly obvious to the psychologist that often we react and behave like animals, and it is sentimental nonsense to expect a man to deny the earthy part of him.

There are people who try to make man something that he is not and succeed only in being ridiculous. I take a dim view of the preaching that all sin is error and that everything is good if we will only say so. We try to live in the hothouse atmosphere of a forced spirituality which is artificial. Whenever I am with one of these other-worldly people for very long, I long for an honest-to-God sinner. We are animals and we are more than animals, but woe unto us if we try to deny our nature. It is a mystery that every once in a while some experience comes to us and we do something that makes us ask in anguish, "Who am I and what is man?"

Jesus Christ is the answer to that question. One of the best things we shall learn from the New Testament is that he was human even as we are. He was tempted at every point even as we are tempted. He walked when he was weary, and he knew the pangs of hunger, thirst, pain. Beware of anyone who wants to rob us of the doctrine of the humanity of Jesus Christ, for he is God's true word to us about who we are. In him God wrote the ultimate word about what man is and what he ought to be.

There was an architect who came up with the brilliant idea that all public rooms ought to be no more than twelve feet high. He said that the high-vaulted ceilings tended to make men feel inferior. He thought we ought to feel at home wherever we are, and therefore we must keep our ceilings low. Dorothy Thompson read that and talked about the GI's she had seen in Salisbury Cathedral, in Canterbury, in Notre Dame, and in St. Peter's. Were they feeling insignificant, she asked, and she answers, "On the contrary they were realizing that life has a grandeur and a beauty and a significance above and beyond themselves that wakened in them high aspiration." Is it for us to bring everything down to our level and decide that the average is to be our example? Not so. It is to rejoice that God gave us a Word to remind us of Him and keep us aware of what our life is meant to be. Jesus Christ is the true sentence, the true word, the "habitual vision of greatness" that finds us when we are lost and restores us when we are weary.

❦ 15 ❧

Wake Up To Reality

Why all this stress on behavior? Because, as I think you have realized, the present time is of the highest importance—it is time to wake up to reality. Every day bring God's salvation nearer.

ROMANS 13:11 (Phillips translation)

THE EARLY Christians lived in a time of great expectancy and crisis. They did not expect the world to last, and they were always talking about the return of Jesus Christ. One would have thought that in that kind of an atmosphere, they would have been sensitive to the great issues of human existence. But even under these circumstances, they had a tendency to lethargy and they grew careless in their behavior. Paul had to call them back from coldness and indifference, and in the words of the Phillips translation he says, "It is time to wake up to reality."

If this was their tendency, it is much more ours. Although we live in a world which stands under the threat of extinction and although our lives are at stake, we grow accustomed to the danger and ignore it. In 1951 Frank Laubach wrote a book entitled *Wake Up or Blow Up*. He sought to make this generation aware of the things necessary for salvation before it is too late. The warning has to be given constantly, for we are prone to let familiarity with danger breed within us a contempt for it. Christians should be those in every generation who are awake to the way things are. Let the Apostle to the Gentiles speak to us and through us.

We may begin with the perfectly obvious assumption that

It Is Easy To Go To Sleep.

We should never assume that we are different from our fathers in this respect and if they drowsed themselves into tragedy, so can we.

Most social revolutions come about because the majority is not aware of what is going on in their society. In 1819 a law was passed in England that no child under nine years of age could work more than twelve hours a day. Even this legislation was passed reluctantly, and there were many members of England's ruling class who saw no need for such special protection for the children of the poor. We look back upon that situation with horror and wonder how men could have been so blind.

Yet there has been revealed to us in our time through pictures and statistical reports, a poverty in what has been called the Appalachian District, of which most of us were totally ignorant. We live in a wealthy society, and most of us are not aware of such pockets of hopeless and degrading poverty. The President's antipoverty program struck many an American as merely a political move because we honestly did not know there was any real poverty in the United States.

Is this not the situation so far as our racial revolution is concerned? We simply assumed that our Negro brethren were making some progress and that things were in fairly good shape. To be aroused by the cry of despair and bitterness has been a great shock to many a white citizen of the nation. We had thought that everybody was more or less content, and now to discover that a tenth of our population has grown desperate because of their segregated bondage, comes to us as a great surprise. We have been asleep, and if we do not awaken to the truth in a hurry, we shall have bloodshed and a division of our people.

This has been characteristic of much of our thought about old age and sickness. The brave words which are spoken of free enterprise and the bitter attack against anything that sounds like "socialism" come from men who are not old and not poor and not sick. Old age for many an American is a time of fear which gradually we are being made to see and recognize. The man who is caught by poverty and illness is not interested in talking political theory. It is too bad the AMA did not learn this simple lesson a long time ago. Let us wake up to the condition of people who are outside our comfortable condition.

We fall asleep personally in so many ways. The spiritual part of life, which we profess is the most significant, becomes merely sentimental and verbal without reality. Religious life begins with a great spiritual experience which gradually runs down and is lost before we know what has happened. It is hard to understand, but it is certainly observable that most of us grow gradually less sensitive to the spiritual demands of life and God.

We fall asleep mentally. Joseph Kennedy, the father of the late President, urged his children to think every day. It was a good word, for it is easy to fall into the drowsy habit of accepting opinions without examining them with our minds. Thought is painful and it often gets us into trouble. But we get into worse trouble when our minds are unresponsive to the challenges of life.

Of course, this is true of us physically, which is why our physical condition becomes of some concern usually when it is too late. We get overweight and we are unable to walk more than a few steps without fatigue because we are armchair athletes. The American way of life seems to be to hire a few young men to play the games for us. We want a contest which we can observe from a comfortable seat in the stadium, or better yet, in an armchair in front of television. Somebody needs to tell us to wake up to the reality of what a man ought to be and what he can become physically, mentally, and spiritually when he falls asleep.

Charles Darwin confessed that after years of concentrating on his science he could no longer listen to music. Sir Robert Walpole picked up a book one time in his library and cried out, "My God, I can't read." He had not lost his sight. But his long involvement in politics to the exclusion of all other interests had robbed him of his taste. It is hardly too much to say that one of the hardest tasks in life is to stay awake.

Another thing we need to note is that

We Create a Dream World That Is Not Real.

It is not only drowsiness that is our problem but a tendency to see things that are not there. Paul's key word in this text is *reality*. What is the true nature of things and what is possible in our world?

In the nineteenth century America went through a period of constructing political utopias. New communities were formed on theoretical foundations. Emerson writing to Carlyle in 1840 said, "We are all a little wild here with numberless projects of social reform. Not a reading man but has a draft of a new Community in his waistcoat pocket. I am gently mad myself, and am resolved to live cleanly. George Ripley is talking up a colony of agriculturists and scholars with whom he threatens to take the field and the book. One man renounces the use of animal food; and another of coin; and another of domestic hired service; and another of the state; and on the whole we have a commendable share of reason and hope." These communities failed, although they sounded so good in theory. Man's constant temptation is to assume that his ideas can be established in spite of the limitations of human nature and the hard reality of social facts.

Social experiments are no new thing, and in our time the great theory has been communism. Its failure was revealed by Russia's vicious attack on the Hungary freedom fighters. It is being revealed by the necessity of bringing communist practice more into harmony with economic reality. The worst enemy of Russia has been the doctrinaire interpreters of what had to happen because Lenin said so. One by one these theories have cracked against the rocks of reality.

Freud was a great mind with some profound insights. But Freud had some curious blind spots, and his interpretation of religion could be called nothing less than childish. On the basis of some observations and many personal prejudices, he constructed a theory of religion as wholly illusory. But in order to construct such ideas he had to ignore great areas of religious history and practice which contradicted his theories. There can be no doubt but that he exploded some fine religious superstitions, but in their place he substituted other superstitions which are no nearer truth simply because he thought they were scientific.

If I am defeated in any attempt, it can work to my good unless I try to alibi the defeat. If I find the wrong reason for it or blame it on the wrong cause, I shall learn nothing from the experience and am doomed to repeat it again. An honest analysis of what went wrong when I failed to attain my goal, will make the disappointment beneficial and hopeful. It is the unrealistic consideration of the true cause of failure that hinders men and makes their progress so slow.

If my weakness is honestly considered and I come to the conclusion that the particular job I am doing demands gifts I do not have, then this is all to the good. It is the continual assumption that my weakness is not weakness and that by simply trying again I can succeed, that condemns me to an endless circle of frustration. The experience of failure is more valuable to us than success if we do not cover it up with sham thinking.

We create a dream world made up of physical pleasures. We picture life with a single dimension and wonder why such a life does not satisfy us. Our ideas of happiness are almost always materialistic and the affluent society is full of personal tragedies because most of us are not realistic about what we want. The main mark of the religious interpretation of life is realism.

When Bishop Francis Asbury of The Methodist Church rode from Maine to South Carolina and from the Atlantic Coast to Ohio and back, he often spent nights in lonely mountain cabins. While he preached to large crowds at times, he often held services for one family. He was ruled by one purpose, which was to bear witness to the meaning of Christ whether he talked to one or a thousand. He writes in his *Journal:* "We must preach the gospel in every kitchen." This is the word of a man who had been where the people are and who knew the human situation. Asbury's preaching revealed no

idealistic world of his own imagining. His word was directed to the
people who found themselves not in a cathedral but in the kitchen.
This kind of preaching every generation needs with its awareness of
the real conditions of ordinary life.

In the third place

We Need To Be Realistic Enough To Look Ahead.

The important thing is the end of the journey, and the goal toward
which all the present actions tend must be in our minds. In religion
the science of last things is called *eschatology,* which is a technical
word describing the importance of judging the present by where it
is leading.

All a man has to do is look at the present situation to know that it
was not born with us. For good or for ill, we are now reaping what
our fathers sowed in the years past. Unless we are completely blind
to our own responsibilities, we shall see that the next generation will
be suffering the consequences of our present decisions. To put it
another way, one of the main contemporary noises is always the
sound of chickens coming home to roost. We can never begin with
the present, for we always live under limitations set by the past.

Decisions made in crisis too often fail to take a long look ahead.
This happened in World War II when agreements were signed and
promises were made which proved to be unrealistic and even foolish
a few years later. There are those in this country who want us to
believe that the President of the United States and his generals were
all subversives and therefore made these decisions with malice of
forethought. This is utter nonsense, and the mistakes made were
natural enough. These men were acting under the pressure of a
people who wanted it all over with immediately and longed for
normal living. Nor should we forget that these decisions were made
when there seemed to be a good chance that the Allies would stay
together during the period of reconstruction and peace.

Now we are aware that some of these agreements were foolish,
and we are hard put to understand the logic of establishing West
Berlin as a little island in the midst of a great communist sea. Hard

political thought should have indicated that this would not work out satisfactorily for very long. But in this we are but illustrating the human tendency to choose a present hope over against the future probability.

At the present time, the experts are deeply concerned over the population explosion. The present situation is tolerable, but we see a future crisis awaiting us. Either we begin to do something about it now or we shall bequeath to the next generations insurmountable problems. If we believe in the sacredness of life and the right of persons to decent opportunities, then we must consider what the present unchecked birth rate means.

This is the great thing about the Bible. It talks to us about last things and it defines the consequences of certain policies. Jesus set down principles of behavior which would lead us to life. It is not so much that the gate we enter now is narrow as of where it leads and what the traveler will find on the straight path tomorrow. Christianity is a way of life which glorifies the present moment and promises a future joy. It is a way of life that says the present suffering is not worthy to be compared with what is prepared for the followers of the Lord Jesus.

Personal habits tend to get rigid without much personal thought or consideration. We have a tendency to drift into certain ways until they become our way of life. Nobody ever started out to become a dope fiend, but our philosophy is to enjoy a present thrill with no concern for the future. One day a man awakens to the horrible truth that he is no longer free and what he has been playing with has now enslaved him. The religious man will fall into no such trap.

The future is shaped by what we commit ourselves to now. The cause that promises an immediate profit and no more is not for realistic people. The men who find life have enlisted in the cause whose fulfillment is a continuing and an enlarging experience. That cause which has no more than a physical promise of comfort or physical thrill is not worthy of much consideration.

The Jewish scholar Theodor Reik wrote a most unusual book entitled *Jewish Wit*. His thesis was that what men laugh at reveals a great deal about them. He collected stories Jews tell about themselves and the humor which came out of great distress. A Jewish boy in Brooklyn came home one day and very excitedly said to his father, "The Yankees were defeated by the Dodgers this afternoon." The father pondered it for a moment and asked, "Is this good or bad for the Jews?" The story reveals a people who must think of every passing event in terms of its good or ill effect on them. This could become too selfish and too self-centered, but it is also a point of view that every man needs to consider. Let us look at the present decision and ask how it will appear in another ten years. Where will this road lead us if we follow it to the end? Every Christian needs to be made aware of the importance of "eschatology" and consider the present experience with an eye on the future.

Finally, let us rejoice that

God in Christ Wakes Us Up to Reality.

Christianity is the most realistic way of life I know. The prophets proclaimed justice because only on the basis of justice can nations live. They looked below the surface of prosperity and described the fate of a society that exploited the poor and enriched the comfortable. The missionary goes abroad to proclaim righteousness in human relations, and the Christian word in any society awakens to reality.

The truth is that the unseen values are the determining ones. Men are blinded by what they can see and touch and forget the transitoriness of such matters. That which no man can see is at work among us and brings to judgment our vaunted success and prosperity. Reality flies away from men who are committed to taking the cash and letting the credit go. The trouble with the so-called practical man is that he is so shortsighted.

We live by affirmations which we cannot prove. We are saved by faith in the reality of God's will and the moral law. The hopes that make us men are the visions of tomorrow given by God. It is this Christian hope of men under God, committed to build a new Jerusalem which defeats cynicism and disillusionment. The love of

Christ constrains us, cures our loneliness, and breaks down our separations. We see hatred, but in our hearts we know love which is stronger than hate. This is the realism which saves us.

The Christian lives in the midst of what is ultimate and essential. He has the long look and the perspective of eternity. Waking up to reality is not growing more pessimistic and hopeless but having our eyes opened to the unseen forces and the spiritual allies. The coming of Christ into a man's life is waking from sleep and being made alert to realities rooted in God.

Some years ago I was visiting in the Fiji Islands and heard the story of John Hunt, a young Methodist missionary from England who converted the cannibal tribes. He writes in his journal about the lying and immorality of the chiefs. He speaks of the stench of burning human flesh when the warriors returned from their raids and prepared for the feast. But he bore his witness bravely and patiently, although when he died in 1848 there was little sign of any general repentance or conversion. But some years after his death the main chief, Thakombau, became a Christian and led a great movement into the church.

One day in a little church on the little island of Baa, I saw a rough stone with the top hollowed out. It was used as a baptismal font. They told me it was the old killing stone upon which Thakombau had killed his victims. It had been stained with human blood. Now the sacrament of baptism is the symbol of entrance into the new life of Christ. And I said to myself, wouldn't it be great if every church could have something to remind the people of what they were in their sin and what they can become when Christ finds them. This symbol of the worst and the best spoke to me that day of the realism of Christianity. Men are bad enough, as God knows, but they are redeemable and we are in the world to bear witness to that truth. Let us wake up to this reality which is the heart of our good news.

❧ 16 ☙

Do Not Be Afraid

Then Jesus said to them, "Do not be afraid; go
and tell my brethren to go to Galilee, and there
they will see me." MATTHEW 28:10

FROM HIS birth until his death a man is battling against fear. He can
never say that he has won a permanent victory, for the enemy comes
back in different guises and under different circumstances. One
problem that has haunted man in every generation is how to deal
with his anxieties.

The Bible makes this very clear. When Adam and Eve had sinned
against the command of God, they fled from him and hid themselves from His presence. The story says, "But the Lord God called
to the man, and said to him, 'Where are you?' and he said, 'I heard
the sound of thee in the garden, and I was afraid . . .'" (Gen. 3:9-
10). The entrance of sin into human life is accompanied by fear.

The prophet Micah, who lived in the eighth century B.C., dreams
of a time of God's rule when all people shall come unto His mountain. There shall be no more war, "but they shall sit every man
under his vine and under his fig tree, and none shall make them
afraid" (4:4). The new age will be the age without fear.

And so we come to the text and note the first words spoken by the
resurrected Lord to the women at the sepulchre. "Do not be afraid,"
he said. The good news is a promise of the conquest of fear. What
Christianity has to offer this generation and all generations is life

lived with confidence and the end of the domination of powers that make men afraid.

Let us begin by suggesting that we are afraid of

The Past.

This will sound like nonsense to some of us, for why should we be afraid of what has already happened? For better or for worse, it is over, and since we have already been through it, surely yesterday cannot arouse fear in us today. This, however, is a very naïve point of view. The past is the breeding ground of the demons of fear.

One of the main difficulties in establishing free nations in Africa is the inability of tribes with long memories to forget their hatreds and their suspicions. It is easy enough to carve out boundary lines, as the colonial powers discovered, but it is not so easy to eliminate tribal memories. It will be a long and painful process before African nations can be set free from the ancient fears.

We sometimes interpret the Russian suspicion of America's relationship with Germany and especially our willingness to rearm Germany as simply an indication of communist intransigence and meanness. But when I visited Russia a few years ago, I came to the conclusion that if I stood in their place I would probably feel very much as they do. They were the victims of a mass invasion by the Nazis who cynically disregarded a treaty signed by Hitler. They saw thousands of acres scorched and hundreds of villages wiped out. I stood one day in Stalingrad and heard a man describe the awful carnage of that turning point in the invasion. Russian flesh and blood withstood the Nazi war machine and endured suffering almost unbearable. No wonder they fear a rearmed Germany and are suspicious of actions which ignore the past.

One of the great things psychology has done for us in our time is to reveal that what happened yesterday is very much alive in our present experiences. There is a sense in which no man outgrows his past and every man lives under the domination of the fear of what happened yesterday. It is amazing to realize that nothing is forgotten and that our lives are being shaped and thwarted by unrecognized experiences of our childhood. We have sought to find some cure for this, and one answer is to assume that all guilt is sickness. If we can drag out these forgotten sources of infection, then we can see how silly they are and be freed of their domination. Sometimes this works and the feeling of guilt can be eliminated if it is only some exaggerated response to a relatively harmless incident. But suppose we feel guilty because we are guilty. What if a man feels that way because it is the truth about him? Suppose guilt is as truly a clue to our nature as innocence. What then?

The Gospel says we must confess our sins and be forgiven by God. The Catholic finds the confessional as a first step on his way to healing, and sometimes the Protestant finds a minister who can help him unload this burden of guilt. But for every Christian there is always God to whom we may confess. He promises us that as far as the east is from the west, so far will he remove our transgressions from us.

A sociologist once made a careful study of embezzlers and labeled them "respectable criminals." Why did these men of good education and family for the most part, steal money from their banks and companies? He found that in nearly every case they had what they believed was an unsharable problem. Unable to talk it over with anyone, they thought they must find a solution by themselves. But the Christian never has an unsharable problem. We can confess our guilt and find release from it.

This is the meaning of the experience of forgiveness. However you may define it and however it may find you, it always comes as a release from the intolerable burden of guilt. If we have been forgiven, we can go on and we can live with ourselves. This is what Christ does for men, and at the heart of the testimonies of the saints you will find this unspeakable joy of being released from the fear of past guilt. Paul knew what it was and tells us that one of his first rules for living was "forgetting those things which are behind." That God helps us do this, is good news, indeed.

A Los Angeles artist specializes in pictures of children misbehaving. She shows them pulling the cat's tail or washing the cat in the salad bowl. She was quite surprised to learn that psychiatrists were buying her pictures and hanging them in their reception rooms, the theory being that a child, upon seeing that other children were also naughty, would be relieved of his guilt feelings. Not much of a solution! Away with such nonsense. Let our burden of past guilt be taken from us by experiencing God's forgiveness through our Lord Jesus Christ.

If we are afraid of the past, we are also afraid of

The Future.

Since World War II our life has been lived in an atmosphere of fear. A kind of hopelessness oftentimes has its way with us as we consider our terrifying problems and our inadequate responses to cope with them. This has been true of young and old, and upon our society has fallen a pall of fear of the future, as gloomy and depressing as a London fog. I was looking at a newspaper headline outside a restaurant in our building, and a man who works in another office stopped and said to me, "Bishop, is it really as bad as it looks?" I told him that as far as it goes, I suppose it was as bad as they described it, but this was only a part of the story. The other part of the story is told to us so softly that sometimes we never hear it.

The extremist groups in America feed on this fear of tomorrow. Instead of ministering to our hope, they try to increase our fear. They tell us that even Presidents of the United States have been agents of a foreign government and we are infiltrated with traitors. This apparently gives them something to live for and makes them feel important, but they are no call to faith and hope. They are the disease and not the healing. And all of their talk is in the name of patriotism. Some patriotism!

If any man begins to think of all that could go wrong with him tomorrow, he will hardly dare to get up in the morning. He can be involved in accidents and he can lose all that he hopes to gain. Begin to think for five minutes about the bad things that might take place and every bit of courage will drain away, leaving only despair and anxiety.

Marriage is a dangerous venture, and it is best undertaken in the days of youth which are days of faith. When men or women wait too long, they will begin to weigh the possibilities of failure against the rather slim chances of success. I have a bachelor friend who is a professor at a theological seminary. When he was told one time that he probably would be elected a bishop of the Church if he were married, his reply was, "But suppose I should get married and then not get elected?" This is not the approach that promises success in marriage or in any other high human adventure.

How can we find a cure for our fear of tomorrow? The Bible finds it by contemplating the greatness of God who makes our petty disturbances comparatively unimportant. So the Bible talks of the God in whose eyes the nations are but a drop in the bucket, and before whom men are as grasshoppers. This is said not to make us small but to make us understand how great God is. Looking down upon the pretenses of the kings and the rulers, the 2nd Psalm says, "He who sits in the heavens laughs; the Lord has them in derision." The Bible is telling us that there is someone in charge of this universe and of our life. Things may seem out of hand to us, but at the last there is a power who rules the world and holds it in His hands.

No one wants to work for a company that has no head. We need to believe that whoever is in charge is a good and able man who will direct the affairs toward success and not failure. The army cannot fight unless it believes in the general. The trouble with the Union armies of the Civil War in the first year was the lack of a man to lead them. Teenage children look back on permissive homes as unhappy places. They feel that permissive parents let them down. Children want some order and direction. The university that turns things over to the students ends up in chaos, with everybody unhappy. The fear of the future is bound up with the fear of no one being in charge.

A senator from a state with a large navy yard was bewailing the fact that the yard was being phased out over a ten-year period. He had fought to keep it but finally confessed that the Secretary of

Defense was the victor. And then he made a most astounding remark. He said, "The one hopeful sign for the yard's future is the
steadily worsening world situation." What a thing to say! Can a
man be so blind as to think that the maintenance of a navy yard
is justified even if a world has to go to war? Thank God Christians
are set free from all such nonsense, for they believe that the future
belongs to God whose will is His children's good. So if yesterday
loses its power of fear over us, so does tomorrow, and we live in the
glad confidence that although God's will may be hindered, it is
never defeated.

In the third place, let us observe that we are afraid of

Life.

We lose our willingness to say yes to the challenges of living and
prefer to be half-alive if it means being safe.

A writer trying to reconstruct the life of the Duke of Wellington
said he was helped most by finding an old account book and
learning how the great man spent his money. He thought this was
more useful than reading speeches made about the Duke or his own
public pronouncements. For the way a man spends his money
indicates what he thinks is important in life.

If a stranger from another planet should suddenly land among us
and look at the budgets of the nations, he would certainly come to
the conclusion that we believe in death but not in life. He would see
us spending billions of dollars for defense and developing instruments of destruction which are out of date almost before they can be
manufactured. He would see the people being heavily taxed to arm
against some enemy, but he would find us too poor to spend adequately for schools, for hospitals, or for the clearance of slums. He
would come to the conclusion that we have lost our confidence in
life. What do you suppose such a one would think about building
bomb shelters and men turning back to live in caves like animals?

What does an examination of the church budget show? Is our
money being spent primarily for housekeeping chores and providing
the institution with comfort and convenience? How much are we

spending for carrying the good news around the world? And just what are we doing in our local communities to make life better? It might be a very good idea for any church to take an objective look at its budget and find out just what it really believes in and what its program is supposed to accomplish.

So far as an individual is concerned, a look at his checkbook stubs would say more about him than his public confession of faith. No matter how unmaterialistic we may claim to be, the way we actually spend our money is probably the best indication of our faith. Back in 1924 a minister listed some news items and compared them with church records. He noticed this in the paper: "Mr. and Mrs. B left last night for New York, where they will attend the World Series. They will be gone about three weeks, during which time they will visit Niagara and other points of interest in that section." When he turned to his church records, he found this: "Mr. B sent his check to the treasurer for $60 covering his annual contribution for the support of the church benevolences. Accompanying it was a note saying that he was sorry it had to be less than last year."

The wife of one of my fine pastors told me they had to tell the children they could not do something they wanted to do because they did not have the money. "Just how poor are we?" asked their daughter. And the mother told her that they were only poor in relation to money, but they were very rich in the things that mattered. Which is what a Christian ought to say and feel, for he has been given new life and is the steward of wonderful possessions.

How shall we be cured of our fear of life? By faith in Christ and not by making any claims of our own merit and worth. By believing that his way, while straight and narrow, leads us to the great and open places of God's concern. Remember how he said that he came that we might have life and have it more abundantly. And to have faith in his way is not to make our living narrow and mean but to make it large and gracious.

We find our hope in Christ who bestows upon us the glad confidence that we are led day by day into the forever-enlarging tomorrows. When the city of Dothan was surrounded by the Syrian army to capture Elisha, the prophet's servant despaired, but Elisha prayed that his eyes might be opened. Then he saw on the mountains the horses and chariots of God. This is the hope which comes to men who have named His name. They see the unseen allies of the human spirit, and the future shines with promise.

Life becomes great through the experience of the love of Christ. We are not talking about the Hollywood kind of love which is so terribly mixed up with lust and egotism. We are talking about our response to God who showers upon us His gifts and who taught us in the Crucifixion that there is no limit to His love. Harriet Beecher Stowe in one of her books says, "And my theology is, once penetrate any human soul with the full belief that *God loves him,* and you save him." Yes, you save him and you introduce him to life.

In the parable of the talents Jesus tells us about the man who left his property with his servants. The servant who had been left five talents earned five more; the servant who had been given two talents earned two more; but the one who had been charged with only one, hid it in the ground and could only return it to his master, saying, "I was afraid." Jesus comes to overcome our fear of living and teach us how to use what God has given us for life.

The assistant superintendent of schools in St. Louis, Sam Shepherd, Jr., says that as a part of their program to change slum children's attitudes, they give them composition assignments. Some time ago the subject was "Why You Should Be Better than You Are." And here is what one fourth-grader wrote: "Why you should be better than you are: I want to be better than I'm are because it don't mak since to be ignut and dum because I want a good education. I want to go all the way through school. I want a good decent job. That's why I'm going to be better than I'm are." One thing is perfectly clear, and that is that the English "are" terrible. But see how this youngster is reaching out for something which he begins to know is worth having. For the first time he is thinking of life as exciting and promising. He can escape the slums. Here is one escaping from fear into life, and this is what Christ does for every man.

Finally, we are afraid of

Death.

Here is the power of the tyrant as he controls people because he controls life. Men are afraid to die, and they will do his will because he can kill them. But if by any chance he finds somebody who is not afraid of dying, he has amazingly little power over him.

Our society is organized on the assumption that people want to live and will do almost anything rather than die. Whenever I am driving down the highway and see cars coming toward me, I realize that all that separates us is a white line. Why am I not afraid that somebody will cross over into my lane unless there is an accident or some fool is driving intoxicated? I am confident because I can assume that he does not want to die any more than I do. Indeed, we are dedicated to the proposition that we must prolong life for just as long as possible, and in a wild desire to make it quantity rather than quality, we make it vulgar and cheap.

Paul makes a marvelous statement to the Philippians. He writes, "For me to live is Christ, and to die is gain. If it is to be life in the flesh, that means fruitful labor for me. Yet which I shall choose I cannot tell. I am hard pressed between the two. My desire is to depart and be with Christ, for that is far better. But to remain in the flesh is more necessary on your account" (1:21-24). Here is the confession of a man who is not afraid to die and welcomes it. But he knows it is his duty to live and continue his work.

What if there is no death? Suppose a man could believe that dying is but an incident and not a finality? What would that do to his life? Suppose that God has dealt with us in such a way that we believe He has set eternity in our hearts not to disappoint us, but to give us a foretaste of what is in store for us? Suppose that there was One who died and rose again that we might know that God intends for us to live in the power of the Resurrection faith. The great thing which I have to say to you is not only that Christ removes our fear of the past, of the future, and of life, but he takes away the fear of death.

An English scholar was traveling in India and saw a poor untouchable woman working in a paddy field under a blazing sun. He asked a missionary friend what an illiterate outcaste like that could really understand of the Christian faith. And the missionary replied, "She understands that Christ is stronger than the demons." He went on to say that she had been the victim of evil spirits and lived in constant fear of demons who threatened her and pursued her every step of the way. Then in Christ she discovered One who was stronger than these demons and she was no longer afraid. She probably would not understand Charles Wesley's great verse:

> He breaks the power of cancelled sin,
> He sets the prisoner free;
> His blood can make the foulest clean;
> His blood availed for me.

But her experience was the same as that which inspired those lines, and it comes to every person, great or small, wise or foolish, who has heard our Lord say, "Do not be afraid." This is the good news for a Christian on Easter and every day.

❦ 17 ❧

Four Books To Live By

> And I saw the dead, great and small, standing be-
> fore the throne, and books were opened. Also
> another book was opened, which is the book of
> life. And the dead were judged by what was writ-
> ten in the books, by what they had done.
>
> REVELATION 20:12

THE AUTHOR of the Book of Revelation thinks in picturesque and dramatic pictures. He believes that a man's character spells out his destiny, and in his picture of the Last Judgment, he describes books being opened. While individuals may have forgotten their deeds, he indicates that everything has been written down, and it is a terrify-ing moment when God looks at the record. So it is, and that is why death is a fearful event for us all. But at the Judgment there is also what Revelation calls "The Book of Life," which is the note of hope and redemption.

It came to me that books play these two parts in our life. They are a judgment upon us and they are also promise and hope. How wonderful are books! Life without them would be almost unbear-able. They criticize us and they encourage us. Said Carlyle in a letter written to a friend, "Blessings on Cadmus, the Phoenicians, or whoever it was that invented books."

Some years ago before flying became common, I took many a long trip on trains between the West Coast and the East. For me it was a time to read and study; from morning till night I was caught up in the world of books, uninterrupted by visitor or phone call. Some-times I would notice people who went into the club car and sat with vacant stares, chain-smoking and chain-drinking. In almost pathetic eagerness they welcomed anybody who would sit down near them and talk. But the conversation betrayed a shallow inaneness which was pitiful. I thanked God that I had learned to read and that I loved books.

Today I want to speak of four books Methodists live by. I do not address my own people in any spirit of exclusiveness or superiority, but only to speak of one of the traditions in the Christian church. First, I want to mention

The Date Book.

Whenever I am away from home and see a man take out of his pocket that little black book which our Publishing House gives to every Methodist preacher, I know who the man is even though I may never have seen him before in my life. Methodists are supposed to take that book seriously, and especially preachers.

Now there are a good many people who think that keeping track of one's appointments is a very great nuisance. They resent the very idea of their life being governed by particular appointments that have to be kept at particular times. When I was in seminary, I remember that some of the students were making the point that it is impossible to expect a man to preach at a certain time on a certain day every week. We pointed out that at times men do not feel like preaching and sometimes they had not been inspired to speak. Preaching by schedule, we said, was to sin against the Holy Spirit. I still recall the old professor who stood it as long as he could and then growled out, "Young gentlemen, you will learn that the ministry consists of doing a good many things at certain times, whether you feel like doing them or not. Woe unto you if your life is governed by the way you feel. You are to stand in your pulpit on Sunday morning and preach the Word to the very best of your ability whether you feel inspired or not." And I want to say to every person who resents the date book as a nuisance to consider the alternative.

Some see a schedule as a taskmaster and rebel against it. These people are always late and never take seriously a set time for a task. They are the kind of people who waste not only their own time but other people's as well, all in the name of their freedom. They do not impress me so much as being free people, but as selfish people who have no consideration for the time and convenience of others. I still think that my time may be about as valuable as theirs.

We may look upon this book as our enemy and engage in a continual war with it. In the name of being more spiritual than others, we may disregard schedules. We shall probably wake up one day and discover how little we have accomplished on this rebellious path and how much time we have spent on things that produced nothing either good or bad.

We need the date book and we need to take it seriously. For the passing minutes are God's common gift to every man, and it is the one place where we are equal. No one has more time than another and one man's advantage over another is only in his willingness to organize his time and use it wisely. John Wesley said when he was a young man that he and leisure had parted company, and he was so concerned with the gift of time that he planned every day.

Let us be aware of the sin of wasted days. I shall not forget an early session of the Council of Bishops shortly after I had been elected to this office. Some of the older brethren spoke of their experiences and tried to give good advice to the neophytes. Bishop G. Bromley Oxnam spoke on files and told us how he kept his records and what forms he had prepared to keep clear all the things a man ought to do. He had a form he sent to wherever he had agreed to speak, which was to be filled out and returned to him. It told him what time the meeting began, how he should be dressed, and what time he might expect to get away. While some of us have never found it possible to follow the path quite that far, it did reveal how he could do more work in his lifetime than ten ordinary men usually accomplish. Sometimes when on my way to a place I cannot remember where, why, or when, I wish I had taken his advice more seriously.

Christians must be aware of themselves as men under orders, and that means they cannot meander around and take all kinds of time for unimportant things. Methodists have a heritage of making the moments count, and we ought to consider the wasting of time as a sin. We do not have to be merely nervous, anxious people in order to become the kind of persons who appreciate the eternal significance of this particular moment. Let me confess that I think the more we learn to live with the date book, the more we shall accomplish and the happier we are going to be.

There was an unfeeling man who said to a little boy without shoes, "If God loves you, why doesn't he tell somebody to give you a pair of shoes?" The boy answered, "He did tell somebody, but somebody forgot." Oh, the harm we do by forgetting things God wants us to do and say. Our best defense against that tragedy is a date book with which we learn to live gladly.

The second book I want to speak of is

The Discipline.

That is the name of the book which contains the legislation and the regulations of The Methodist Church. While much of church polity has to be assumed and experienced, still the main things can be written down. We are a people who believe that so far as possible, we ought to have these matters spelled out for us so that we are never in doubt about our rights, our privileges, and our obligations.

The temperament which rebels against this interpretation of a church will probably always be restless within our fellowship. John Wesley, for example, had no real appreciation or admiration for the mystics. He felt, for one thing, that they had no proper appreciation for the Church and were as a result too much individualists. But I think that he resented also the idea of an undisciplined religious experience which refused to bring itself under the criticism of the fellowship. He felt more at ease when he saw things spelled out and submitted to the judgment of his reason.

Today as in all times there are a good many people who rebel against rules and regulations governing the church. Indeed, there are some who think that the church must be eliminated if we are going to do what needs to be done. Much of the modern talk about church "renewal" seems to be obsessed by the idea of destroying the institution. We need to be renewed daily, but not by way of eliminating the organization which if destroyed today would have to be rebuilt tomorrow. Institutions are society's way of preserving its treasures and passing them on to the future. Institutions need critics, but the cry to go back to the unorganized, spontaneous way of the early Christians is nonsense. It is not possible, and even if it were, it would not be desirable.

We have seen a renaissance of the so-called "speaking in tongues" movement. It seems to me to be the obvious fact that if we judge things by their fruits, this movement does not come out well. It is a desire for an undisciplined spontaneity which leaves to each individual the right to behave as he pleases. This is no new thing, and the church has always had to find some form of discipline to control it and discourage its excesses since the days of St. Paul. Which is to say that there is always a spirit among us that is unfriendly to the idea of discipline in the church.

But this book we are considering is really to set us free. The older I have grown, the more I have come to appreciate the Methodist *Discipline* as an almost perfect balance between authority and liberty. It works for both the preacher and the layman, telling each one where his responsibility is and what his freedom is. We can use it in a ridiculous way, of course, but when we see it in its proper perspective, it is a very present help in time of trouble for both minister and laity.

The preacher sometimes thinks that the book is a barrier to prevent him from doing what he wants to do. Sometimes it is. But when there is a real issue raised and a real conflict occurs, he will often find the book his best defense. I have noticed that ministers tend to ignore it or look down upon it until there comes a time of real crisis, and then they discover its value.

The same thing is true of the laity. I have heard that they sell more *Disciplines* to laymen in the Philippine Islands than anywhere else in the world. This is not altogether a good thing, for sometimes the result is bickering and division which prevent constructive action on the part of the Church. Today a good many Christian churches are beginning to discover the laity and to emphasize the layman's role in preaching the Gospel, but Methodists have had a pretty clear idea of this matter for a long, long time. Now and again a man finds real inspiration in discovering that his church has established his position and his importance.

When I was leaving the Portland Area of our church some years ago, some of the brethren had a dinner for me. The president of the Council of Churches made a speech. He was a Congregational layman and a great churchman in every way. He said some things about Methodists that intrigued me and helped me to see our church in a clearer light. As I recall, he said that Methodist preachers had always been somewhat of an enigma to him. They are to me, for that matter. But his observation was that they seem to combine two opposite things in their behavior. For one thing, he said they were men who went where they were sent without complaint and spent no time in candidating for a particular pulpit. (The brother was a little naïve on this point.) Yet, he went on, if there was a conflict in the community involving social and moral values, you could be fairly sure that the Methodist preacher would be right in the center of it. They were men, he thought, who on the one hand were disciplined and on the other hand free. They were under orders, yet they were independent. It came to me that the purpose of discipline is to set us free. Whether or not we would agree with that man's estimate of Methodist preachers, at least this is the theory and the aim of a church that is supposed to live by a book called *The Discipline.*

There is an old story about a little boy whose mother gave him two nickels one Sunday morning and told him that one was to go into the Sunday School offering and the other was his to spend as he pleased. Walking down the street and feeling very affluent, he was tossing one of the nickels into the air when he dropped it. The coin rolled off the gutter into a drain and was lost. The boy looked very sad for a moment, and then he brightened up and said, "Well, Lord,

I lost your nickel." He speaks for many Christians who give God whatever is left over and expect Him to suffer the main losses. Disciplined Christians will exhibit no such behavior and will learn to understand that there are some things which the Lord does demand of us. Let us be glad of this second book which we are to live by and let us be glad it is called *The Discipline*.

The third book is

The Hymn Book.

Hymns are an important part of all Christian worship, but they are of particular significance for Methodists. Charles Wesley wrote over six thousand hymns and was one of the great hymn writers of all time. We have been noted for our congregational singing from the beginning. Indeed, when, or perhaps I should say if, I get to heaven, I am going to ask that Gabriel call all the Methodists together and have them join in "O For a Thousand Tongues to Sing My Great Redeemer's Praise." To hear a Methodist Conference open with the brothers and sisters singing "And Are We Yet Alive?" is the sweetest music this side of heaven. When Methodist congregations begin to keep silent instead of lifting their voices in song, then we know there is something radically wrong with us and we have indeed lost the way.

Have you ever considered how important music is to any good cause? Is it true that men on crusades always sing? Take the crusade for civil rights in our time, for example. One of the first things they did was find a song, and whenever you have a civil rights crowd together they will soon be singing, "We Shall Overcome." When men are really on the march and have a great hope and a great conviction, they sing. The right to vote is decided by Congress, but the power of the movement is to be found in the singing crowds.

The labor unions in the early days sang. They did not meet just to hold business sessions, for they were a crusade. Some of those old songs still bring back nostalgia to many a veteran from the labor movement who has not heard them for a long time. This in itself tells something about what has happened to this cause. Harry Golden once remarked that he never heard the NAM singing at their meetings. Believe me, you can tell a great deal about what kind of an organization it is by simply asking whether or not they know how to sing.

Methodists have been people who put their hymn books side by side with their Bibles. Our English brethren have no hesitancy in quoting a Wesley hymn to illustrate a doctrine or to give a Methodist interpretation of Christianity. For the great things of our faith are beyond logic, and they have never depended on the fine points of reason. Our theology is sung, and that is the best way to treat theology.

Not all of us are poets, and there are a good many of us these days who cannot appreciate what passes for modern poetry. But poetry is in the soul of man. That which he feels deeply and has assurance about, demands a poetic form for its expression and can never be said in prose. Religion puts its highest and best expressions in poetic form because it is ever pointing man upward from what he knows to what he dares to believe.

Life is never completely a matter of logic, and the perfectly logical approach to reality will lead us only part way. Life is a matter of undefinable feelings, and although I think that Matthew Arnold was wrong when he limited religion to thought tinged with emotion, at least he was moving in the right direction.

The hymn book brings to us the power of joy and the realization that at the heart of the universe there is music. We deal with tragedies, and the Cross reminds us of certain stark facts which no man can escape. But ours is an experience which takes us beyond tragedy, and along with such prosaic things as a date book and a discipline, we possess the hymnal.

The poet Heinrich Heine one time said, "The music at a marriage always reminds me of the music of soldiers marching to battle." This is in some ways a very unfortunate analogy, but in a deeper sense, it is a good one. Marriage is not merely a sentimental affair. When two people join hands at the marriage altar, they are beginning a long, long struggle and they are enlisting for life. They will have all kinds of enemies to meet and all kinds of foes to overcome. They have precious things to defend and preserve. But let there be music in their marriage and let there be music in the church. Methodists have a great treasure in their hymn book.

Finally, we join all Christians in putting first among our books,

The Bible.

I was at a meeting not long ago, and like most of these affairs, the brethren decided they had to set the time for another. Some of them thought it was important that I should be there, and so we began to reach for our date books. To my embarrassment, I had forgotten my date book and in its place I had brought my New Testament. This seemed to make quite an impression, and I was able to say that significant as a date book may be, it is more important to carry your Bible.

I attended a meeting of the California State Board of Education, and in the midst of a dull lecture we were hearing from a professor on how to teach history, there stood out one sparkling idea which I have not forgotten. He said the main problem was to teach children that history was not something embalmed but something contemporary—that the people of history are not bloodless abstractions but are real folks not different essentially from us. And I said to myself that this is what the Sunday School has been doing all the time and we never appreciated it. The Sunday School teaches history from the standpoint of the Bible, and the Bible gives us the sense of being a part of things from the beginning. Amos, Micah, Jeremiah, Isaiah, David, the Disciples, Paul, and Jesus are real to us, for through them we become aware of the God who walks among men in every land and in every age.

The philosopher organizes knowledge into systems of thought, and that is necessary. No one ought to play down what the philosopher does for us in straightening out our thinking and revealing our illogical assumptions. But the Bible does more than that for us because it makes us understand the personal values involved in every situation and the personal conflict in every crisis. Systems of thought are abstractions, but the Bible deals with the reality of persons.

We are in danger of assuming that nothing is any good that is not modern. We pride ourselves on our advancement over our fathers in so many ways. One Sunday morning I left Los Angeles by jet plane to fly to Phoenix. I had a good breakfast aboard and in forty-five minutes I was in Phoenix. I was able to meet with some laymen and ministers and then preach at our Methodist Church in Scottsdale, consecrating the new sanctuary at the close of the service. I greeted the people and then took a plane for Los Angeles, and I was in my home again by half past three. My father, who was a local preacher in the Methodist Church, could never have done that, for he traveled by horse and buggy to his preaching appointments in northern Michigan many years ago. But it came to me that I was bringing the same good news to my congregation he brought to his. The need of his generation is the need of mine. The Bible is as fresh today as it was a thousand years ago.

The great testimony of the Bible is that God speaks to people. He speaks in such a way that we do not always understand Him, and we need to be humble enough to check our hearing with the testimony of the church. But the assurance is there, and if a man listens, he will hear His voice.

The Bible tells us that God works with men and through men. We are not automatons, nor were the men who wrote the Bible. Part of their personality is in it and part of their interpretation is there, so that an extreme literalism becomes ridiculous. But the Bible is the Word of God which men heard according to their ability and wrote down to the best of their skill.

That God is involved in our affairs, is the testimony of the Book. This is the heart of the good news, and whenever we grow discouraged or fearful, we can find courage in remembering that we are not alone. Let no man feel hopeless so long as he has his Bible, for in some strange and wonderful way that Book is not only an ancient testimony but it is a contemporary comfort. One has the feeling that here he is not only reading about something that has happened before, but he is reading about something that is happening now and something that will happen tomorrow.

We were traveling through the Middle East one autumn. We began at Beirut and went down through Lebanon, Syria, and Jordan to Jerusalem. We hired a car and a guide whose name was Jacob. He was an elderly man with great knowledge and a fine Christian spirit. I asked him one day how many languages he knew, and he told me that he could speak eight. And then he added something I have never forgotten. "But," he said, "the main thing for a guide to know is his Bible."

Surely this is the word with which we ought to close. There are so many books in the world, and the man who wants to understand his time will need to read many of them. But there are four of them he had better pay particular attention to if he is a Methodist Christian. They are the date book, the *Discipline,* the Hymnal, and the Bible. But the greatest of them all is the Bible.

❦ 18 ❧

He Did Not Quit!

I have fought the good fight, I have finished the
race, I have kept the faith.   II TIMOTHY 4:7

THIS IS one of the most familiar texts in all the Bible, and I have
been quoting it ever since I was in Sunday School. When I got to
seminary I discovered that the scholars had raised some questions
concerning the Pastoral Epistles and that it was not certain that
Paul had written all that is in them. Such questions used to bother
me more than they do now because I have concluded that much
more important than who wrote a book is the question of whether
or not it is true. Then if you decide that it is true, you need to ask
what the implication is for your own life. I suggest to you that these
words sum up Paul's life and they make a fitting obituary for his
ministry. I think I would be happier to have these words spoken of
my life when it comes to a close than almost anything else that
could be said.

As we grow older we come to see how important it is to hold on.
What Paul is saying here is simply that he did not quit. Such a
sentiment is hardly ever spectacular or dramatic. We are much more
impressed with sudden brilliance or isolated acts of genius. But
finally most things come down to fighting the fight, finishing the
race, and keeping the faith. The Bible puts a very high estimate on
people who do not quit.

I speak to all men when I quote this text. There is not a one of us who has not finally faced the temptation to run away. Sometimes we have yielded and sometimes we have not. But as we look back, those moments when we stayed with the job are the ones we remember with increasing appreciation. Every minister counsels with people who find it difficult to make an honest survey of their past. But if they can, they are surprised to learn that staying with it a little longer was the crucial decision. What a wonderful thing it is for Paul to say that whatever else he may have done or failed to do, he did not quit.

Let us begin by observing that

Life Is the Long Pull.

Paul was using the figures of the arena and the race. Many a man is good at running dashes, but straining forward toward the goal when exhausted is another matter.

Civilization is not attained by a single decisive battle or a brief sudden effort. Civilization is a matter of the long pull and of millions of unknown, faithful people consolidating the gains that have been made and preserving them. There are with us always the savages who would take us back into the jungle. While traveling in the Middle East, I visited the city of Byblos, whose Phoenician name originally was Gebal. It is one of the most ancient cities we know about and was thriving more than four thousand years before the birth of Christ. Here the cedars of Lebanon were shipped to build Solomon's Temple, and it was the center of the papyrus trade, hence the word *Bible* from Byblos. Indeed, when one travels in the Middle East, he comes to think of Roman times as fairly recent. The Crusaders seem to have been there but yesterday. The traveler gets a new idea of what a long time it has been developing a civilized life. Something in men has driven them on and persisted in spite of all the setbacks of war and disease.

We remember Adolf Hitler's boast that he would build a Reich that would last a thousand years. He missed it by a considerable margin, and his words reflected a complete misunderstanding of what a society is and how one goes about building a culture. It takes a good deal more than a military machine, for the experiences which create a culture are slow in developing. Nor are they easily overthrown once they have been established. The memory of free men is a very difficult thing to uproot, which Hitler found to his cost. Deep in the customs of a people there are built those habits and attitudes which are below the surface and which are not quickly cultivated. Neither are they uprooted in a hurry.

We have a tendency to pick out a few crucial events in the birth of a nation as if it could all be summed up in a few happenings which are dwelt upon every Fourth of July. But if you read American history carefully, you will discover that the battles had to be fought on the outskirts as well as at the center of the struggle. Read again the story of George Rogers Clark and the suffering which he and his men endured on the Mississippi. Not every battle is remembered and not every expedition is included in the history books. Always there are those people who in their own way and in their own place are strengthening the good and fighting the evil. Nations have their roots in the patience of many men and women of whom it can be said, "They did not quit."

Any good cause will have an appeal to many persons who certainly prefer goodness to evil. If the engagement is going to be a short one, any number of people will enlist. But great causes are never easily attained, and the short-termers are of very little value when it comes to the final victory. A friend of mine who has been active in community reforms all his life told me one time that it was very easy to get preachers to sit on the platform when the program was launched; but those who will stay with it to the end and do the hard and wearing day-by-day work are few.

The world is full of dramatic starters, but so often they are disappointments. Every pastor knows the laymen who are good for a quick shot in the arm for any Christian enterprise. Ask them to make a speech or chair a short-term committee and they will do fine. But if the church is engaged in any long enterprise, do not depend upon these brethren for leadership. Many of us are willing to lend our names to a good cause, but to give our faithful service until it is achieved is not so common. Most of us looking back over our lives are filled with despair at the number of times we started great things and never saw them through.

So it is that usually less gifted men who have finishing power are the ones who do the work. This does not mean that the able man is doomed automatically to short-term adventures, but it is a familiar pattern. I have known a few men in my lifetime who were brilliant and faithful, but as a general principle, the gifted men were temperamentally unfit to finish the job. This is what makes St. Paul's example so rare and makes us believe that God put His hand upon him in a wonderful way. With the kind of mind that comes along only once a century, he still was the faithful missionary who seems never to have lost his enthusiasm nor his will to finish the course.

Lord Kelvin was one of the great scientists of his time. In the latter part of the nineteenth and the early part of the twentieth century, he contributed to thermodynamics and to the understanding and use of electricity. He received honors from several universities and from the government for his achievement. A statue was erected to him in Glasgow in 1913, and yet he said one time, "One word characterizes the most strenuous of the efforts for the advancement of science that I have made perseveringly during fifty-five years: that word is failure." Which is to say that his success came out of perseverance, or if we may put it the negative way, he succeeded because he did not quit.

Now if we may look at the other side of the coin, we may simply say that

One of Our Continuing Temptations Is To Quit.

Life is so constructed that we are constantly under this pressure. For very seldom do things move so swiftly and satisfactorily that we do not feel ourselves betrayed.

We start out with great enthusiasm, which is one of the signs of youth. Certainly a burden older people have to bear is listening to young people define the issues and describe how easily they can be solved. Parents must endure this experience with their children and try to warn them as gently as possible that it will not be as easy as they think. Professors must listen to students who are never again as bright as they are when they have drunk the heady wine of new knowledge. To youth the whole mess of the world is due simply to older people who grew weary, lost their first enthusiasm, and finally became corrupt. What man among us does not remember the difficulty of understanding the talk of our elders who seemed to be forever counseling patience and compromise.

Yet the time comes when we begin to see that not all of this talk was due to weariness tinged with cynicism. The whole affair was more complicated than we realized, and vitality which is not undergirded with stubbornness is not much good. We will not go very far without enthusiasm, but neither will we go very far if that is all we have.

What is more wonderful than a young man and woman beginning their marriage adventure? They are so much in love and nothing is impossible. Not for them will the experience go sour, and they never doubt but that at the end of the day they will achieve something that never appeared before on land or sea. Yet, the statistics tell a sad story of how many of these confident beginnings end up in a divorce court. There comes a day when there are a hundred reasons why they should quit over against the one reason why they should presevere.

I take great delight in asking young people what they are going to be when they grow up. Ask a ten-year-old boy and you hear a description of a profession or a job he talks about with shining eyes. Yet in my ministry I have met so many people who started out bravely on a high road and lost their way. There was always a good enough reason for it, but finally it comes down to the task demanding a patience which they did not possess.

No one who has lived very long finds it in his heart to blame people who quit. There are always many reasons why it happened, and they are usually good ones. A man's friends will betray him, and in the bitterness of the moment, he gives up in despair and runs from his job. Who can expect a man to be faithful to his calling if other men are not faithful to their vows of friendship?

We have all had promises made to us which were denied. Sometimes life itself seems to dangle a great hope before us, only to dash it to the ground when we reach out to grasp it. Somebody told us how marvelous it would be, and we have found it quite otherwise. Perhaps the whole thing is a sham and nothing we have been told can be believed. In the darkness of such a moment, we quit.

We might have the courage to continue if we could be sure of the ultimate success. Ah, there is the rub! There comes a day when the whole enterprise seems to be in doubt and the outcome trembles in the balance. We do not know that at the end of the road we shall find what we are seeking. We cannot be sure this continued sacrifice will mean victory. We only know that we grope in the darkness for hopes which seem to grow dimmer as we approach them. Enthusiasm ebbs away and doubts have their way with us. There may be now and then some person who does not go through these experiences but who finds life giving him what he wants immediately. But that is not the experience of the vast majority. The cost has a way of rising to frightening heights, and the reward fades away on the horizon.

Some years ago when Adlai Stevenson was defeated for the presidency, I remember that late at night he appeared on television to concede his defeat and speak a few words. It was a hard time for him, but the words he quoted described an experience that many men have had to face. Said Stevenson, "I am too old to cry and it hurts too much to laugh." Most of us will go through such periods not once but many times. We are ashamed to cry, and to laugh demands more than we have. No wonder that so many people give up the fight, drop out of the race, and lose their faith.

Now this situation leads me to the obvious conclusion that

We Need Help.

As long as I can keep this in mind there is hope for me. It is when a man believes he can define the issues by himself and come to his own conclusions that he is in real danger. We need Someone to make us aware of duty which, as the poet said, is the stern voice of God.

It has been my hard experience since I have been a bishop to deal with a good many divorce situations in ministers' families. Most of them follow a pattern so exact that I can almost forecast what a man and his wife will say to me. Whichever one is anxious for the divorce usually begins by saying that they never were in love with the other one. This is obviously nonsense. But they have made themselves believe now that from the very beginning they were misled and were destined to divorce. Then they begin to tell you why they feel obligated for the sake of the children to break up the marriage. Surely it is unfair for youngsters to be in a home where there is quarreling between the parents and where love has died. Is it not the best thing for all concerned that they should set their children free from a loveless home? The third step is usually an announcement that they understand more about the love of God now than they ever did before, and they will be better persons. The minister argues seriously that he will be a better minister because he is going to divorce his wife.

Well, I listen with as much sympathy as I can muster, but I have heard it all before and I do not believe it. For one reason or another they have decided that their patience is at an end and they want a new relationship with somebody else, or they want to make sure that their fading youth is not finally gone. All the time it seems to me obvious that they are not thinking straight nor are they being honest. Have you discovered how much help we need to be honest and how, left to our own devices, we can find so many high-sounding reasons for doing what we want to do? It is easier to quit than to reach for the more difficult solution of working through mutual problems and honoring marriage promises.

Let us realize that we are all having a hard time. I do not know anyone who finds life easy, for with all the comfort and affluence of our modern civilization, personal life does not get any easier. We are in great need of a strength not our own to persevere in the daily difficulties and disappointments of living.

It seems to me that here we discover one of the great responsibilities of the Church. We need a fellowship to encourage us, and we need to be reminded constantly of our moral and spiritual obligations. The Church, when it is truly the redeeming fellowship that it ought to be, keeps us close to the source of our power and makes us aware of the distant goals. As alcoholics often find redemption through a group, so every Christian needs the fellowship of people who are aware of the unseen forces of God. The preacher ought to recognize that his job is to tell people where their help is.

We have a tendency to get too proud and too unsympathetic with our brethren. Character is primarily staying power, and if we are not careful, we shall despise the brother who yields to his weakness. Every now and again, I face things that are too much for me, as if God were reminding me that with all my advantages, I am in constant danger. When this happens I have a new appreciation for the foibles of my brethren and the weakness of my friends. For there is more excuse for them than there is for me, and how many times I find myself at the edge of despair.

Jesus would have no part in promising people that it was going to be easy. Indeed, we are sometimes shocked at the way he cooled down enthusiasm and insisted that men count the cost. If it was possible, he wanted it understood that nobody should follow him without being aware that it was no easy path. He would have had no sympathy with our modern tendency to make it all look effortless.

Many a time I have thought of Demas as the patron saint of our world. Interestingly enough, the reference to Demas comes in the same book and in the same chapter as Paul's great confession of faith. Paul writes, "Do your best to come to me soon. For Demas, in love with this present world, has deserted me and gone to Thessalonica . . ." (II Tim. 4:9-10). He had his reasons, no doubt, but so had Paul. The difference was in Paul's realization that there was help promised by the Christ he had promised to serve.

Francis P. Chisholm one time put down as Chisholm's first law of human interaction, "If anything can go wrong, it will." Then he said there was a corollary of that law which read, "If anything just can't go wrong, it will anyway." Most of us have experienced this truth, and we have lived enough to know that there is not much hope for us in our own strength. We must have help beyond ourselves.

The final word to be said is

Our Hope Is in the Gospel.

What Paul found we can find, and sometimes the only thing that saves us is a willingness to wait a little longer for God to act.

We must learn to live one day at a time. This is Jesus' teaching which becomes more realistic with every new experience that comes to us. If we look too far ahead, we shall then be tempted to seek some way out. But if we can get through today, there will be fresh strength for tomorrow.

A few years ago I had come to a new place to do my work and I was discouraged. The future looked black and forbidding, and it seemed to me as if I would have to spend my time caught up in a hundred obligations that weighed me down. Added to this there was the depressing presence of what we call "smog." My eyes wept and my heart was heavy. An old friend called me up and asked me how things were going, and like a fool I told him. I described all my complaints. He listened for a little while, and then he began to picture the possibilities of the future and the hopes which were waiting to be realized. When he had finished, I said, "You make me feel a little bit better. I will stay until noon." That was the last time I ever felt quite so low about my job and I learned a lesson. Can I make it until noon? If I can I will go that far at least before I quit.

It is amazing how many of the troubles which loom so large as we look far ahead, never materialize. God is always visiting us with divine surprises and miraculously eliminating some of the obstacles in our way. If I can finish the day, tomorrow will have some fresh light which will illuminate the dark picture.

It is good news indeed that he who walks with Christ is kept faithful to the end of the fight. We do not walk alone, and in that desperate moment when we begin to define a hundred reasons why we should desert, we can hold out a little longer if we can see again the great resources of power He has given us. Christians through the years have testified that they are upheld by Everlasting Arms. While there are very few St. Pauls among us, there are thousands who can testify that the same power which saved Paul, saves them.

I visited a religious kibutz in Israel in the fall of 1964. I met there a young Jew and his wife who described what they had been through since the founding of the cooperative years before. They had gone through the War of Independence together, and they had lived without water except what could be brought in from miles away. They lived for years in dirt and hunger. But now it looked so different. Crops were planted and orchards were growing. Roads were black-topped to keep down the dust, and a beautiful new synagogue had been constructed. These were people who had come to that desert land from cultural centers in Europe and had been forced to endure suffering and privation. But they had not quit. They had built something so wonderful that I saw in them the Jewish people at their best, and in them was the embodiment of St. Paul and his heroic perseverance. And I realized again that in the twentieth century as well as in the first century, God gives His children perseverance and patience and courage. With Christ we will fight the good fight, finish the race, and be kept strong by our faith.

❦ 19 ❧

There Came One Running

Good Teacher, what must I do to inherit eternal
life?   MARK 10:17

THE STORY of the rich young ruler has always been one of my
favorites. It has a constant sense of freshness and reality, and it
speaks to me with directness and authority. It begins with great
promise, for Jesus did not make the first approach, but the young
man came to him running. Surely nothing but good can come from
an encounter with Jesus when a man takes the initiative. We have
the feeling that he is serious in his quest and he has a high respect
for the integrity of our Lord. He seems certain that Jesus can give
him the answer to his question. This is the kind of situation that
preachers hope for, and it must have pleased Jesus. Here was the
kind of young man the story says that Jesus loved. Everything is
promising.

Yet in spite of this good beginning, the story comes to a tragic
ending. When the conditions are placed before him, the young man
cannot accept them. When he hears the answer, it involves too
much. The end of the story says, "At that saying his countenance
fell, and he went away sorrowful; for he had great possessions."
What started off with such promise ends with such great disappointment. I am convinced that the incident has within it important
insights for us.

Let me begin by saying that

His Situation Was Similar to Ours.

If I were to choose a person to symbolize this American generation, I would choose the rich young ruler. There is no better example in the New Testament of what we are, what we possess, and what we lack.

For one thing, he was rich, and that of course impressed his contemporaries. The big gap between poverty and riches was greater then than it is now, and he stood out in his world as having great possessions. He was young, and we have a great admiration for youth. Here is no middle-aged or elderly man coming to repent for wasted years. Everything is before him, and the right word will start him on a great career. That such a serious purpose should characterize a young man seems all to the good. How can anything go wrong?

The New Testament says he was a "ruler," which must have meant that he was a man of importance and standing in the community. He had status and he commanded respect. He was the kind of person advertisements talk about when they offer us gifts for "the man who has everything."

Turn now to our situation and see how similar he was to us. Think of the riches we possess and we shall see that as this young man stood out from his society, so we stand out from the whole world. This came home to me a good many years ago when my wife and I were taking a bicycle trip through England. We met a city official in Plymouth, and for some reason or other he invited us to his home. I remember in the course of the conversation that he brought up automobiles and asked me if I had a car. At that time I was in my first church after seminary and I was receiving a salary of fifteen hundred dollars a year, and there was no parsonage. I mentioned that I owned a Plymouth and he was much impressed. He told me that it took a great deal of money in England for a man to own and drive a Plymouth. I shall never forget how amazed I was that a young preacher in his first year in the ministry would be regarded as well-to-do in England.

Since that time I have had the privilege of visiting with Methodist preachers in South America, in Europe, in Asia, in Africa, in Australia, and in New Zealand. One thing I have learned is that all of these men would consider themselves rich if they were receiving the minimum salary of the Southern California–Arizona Conference. Surely it is noteworthy that a Methodist preacher in our country is regarded as a wealthy man in most other parts of the world. Indeed, we are rich.

He was young and we have a great admiration for youth. We are a young nation, and with the exception of a few extremists, we are looking toward the future and not the past. Unlike some other civilizations, we have no great respect for age and its experience. The worst possible thing is for us to look old and act old, so we employ all kinds of subterfuges to cover up the marks of the passing years. We set the retirement age ever earlier, and American business puts its confidence in youth. The Church wants young ministers, so that sometimes I remind church committees that there is a law against shooting a preacher when he is sixty. But the universal cry is for young men and let someone else worry about the older ones. Beauty parlors and their products are high on the list of necessities for modern women. The main thing is to look and act young, even if it kills us.

We have great power and prestige around the world. Our decisions affect millions beyond our borders. We need enough imagination to realize what it is to be a part of a society whose very existence depends upon other people's choices. To be an American is to be where the influential decisions are made. So that altogether we would have to say as it was said of the young man, we are rich, we are young, and we are influential.

In the eighteenth century when Robert Walpole was Prime Minister of England, he gave his report to the Queen one year with considerable satisfaction. "Madam," he said, "there are fifty thou-

sand men slain this year in Europe, and not one Englishman."
Something of that same spirit is ours when we can say that there are
millions of hungry people in the world but not one American; there
are millions of poor people but we are not poor. Yes, in many ways
the rich young ruler is the symbol of us and our successful way of
life.

In the second place, this young man speaks to us because

He Needed a Purpose for Living.

In spite of everything he possessed, he was poor. In spite of all his
good fortune, he was miserable. A society that finds tension increasing and simple happiness harder to achieve will understand something of his state of mind.

Now the rich young ruler is not a man who is down and out.
Here is no moral leper shunned by decent people. This is no
prodigal son reduced to feeding the swine. Indeed, he can make a
most remarkable statement when Jesus tells him that the Ten
Commandments must be kept. He says without any embarrassment
and apparently without any hypocrisy that he has kept them from
his youth up. He is not an alcoholic, nor has he fallen under the
control of some evil habit which is destroying him. He is clean-cut,
moral, and beyond reproach in his living.

He seems to be competent in handling his own affairs. He is not
an outcast who cannot adjust himself to his station in life, but seems
to have done very well. There is no sign that he was one of those
sensitive young men who find it impossible to adjust to the hard
practical things of life. He gives every appearance of being at home
in his world and quite able to fill his position in an exemplary way.
He was, in a word, a successful man, and that is something we can
understand and something we can admire. If you had asked anyone
in the crowd that day, he would have said that this fellow had
everything that men need to be content. The world had treated him
very well. But in spite of it all, he was unhappy and miserable.
Somehow life had bogged down and somehow the future had no
promise and no hope.

C. G. Jung said that a good many people who came to consult him for help, described their situation by simply saying, "I am stuck." This predicament was his, and it is ours. Joseph Wood Krutch, the critic and moralist, said in an article that ours is an age of fun. We have dedicated ourselves to having a good time and amusing ourselves. Certainly it is true that those who sell recreational equipment are doing a tremendous business. We buy motor boats and spend the weekends running them on the oceans, the rivers, and the lakes. We learn all kinds of sports. If we do not want to participate, at least we can sit in the stands and watch somebody else play the games. Our urban civilization makes it possible for us to enjoy sophisticated amusement whenever we desire it.

Yet as Krutch points out, it is not only an age of fun but it is also an age of violence and despair. These things seem to be quite contrary and inexplainable. Why is it that they all come together in the same society? He says that if you seek fun too persistently, you discover that you cannot possibly have it all the time and this leads to boredom. The truth is that such a purpose is not good enough for men and in their disappointment, some despair, and others turn to violence. The streets of our cities become unsafe for people to walk on after dark, not because men are poor, but because men are not having any fun. The Chicago Chief of Police said some time ago that if the present trend continues, Michigan Boulevard will not be a safe place for pedestrians. So it turns out that men who have the leisure and the money to make amusement their goal turn at last to violence just for the sake of violence.

I believe that the extremism of the far right is produced by this lack of purpose. For who are these people anyway? Often they are individuals who are not very prominent, and to join a secret society and hate folks gives them a sense of being involved in something important. How else could a retired candy manufacturer become known? People who can form a kind of conspiracy against the majority have the same childish joy as boys forming a secret club or girls organizing a secret sorority. The tragedy of the whole extremist movement is its witness to a way of life that has found no constructive purpose worthy of men who must give as well as receive.

A Polish psychologist by the name of Dabrowski throws a kind of bombshell into our modern theories of human behavior. He says that dissatisfaction and disharmonies within ourselves are not necessarily signs of sickness but signs of growth. He suggests that the man who feels neurotic and anxious is being urged by a power not himself to move on to a new plateau of health. The answer, he says, is not in trying to adjust ourselves on the level where we are now, but to heed these spurs that would drive us upward and forward. If I were to put it into religious terms, I would say that it all means that God will not let us be content with animal comforts alone but fills our hearts with a great emptiness until we are seeking what the young man called "eternal life."

John Fischer, editor of *Harper's Magazine,* traveled in Iran, the modern name for Persia. He commented on the suspicion and distrust which permeates that society so that nobody really trusts anybody else. He says that in the cities there are empty lots surrounded by walls, for the first thing a man has to do is build a wall around anything he owns. Sometimes when the wall is built the man has no money left to build the house, and so in the cities are these empty, walled-in places. And I thought to myself that this is typical of many lives. We have possessions which we wall in to protect, but they are only empty spaces. We want and we need more than this to live for. Like the rich young ruler, we have everything and we have nothing.

This leads to the third point, which is that

He Recognized His Personal Responsibility.

In this, of course, he differed markedly from us, and here he has something very important to teach us.

Something that impresses me very much today is a growing lack of personal responsibility for what happens to us. If you read the contemporary novels, you must be impressed with a general spirit of blamelessness which fills most of them. Here are people portrayed living like pigs and then very much upset when they begin to feel like pigs. There is never any indication that this stale, corrupt life is any fault of the people themselves, but on the contrary, they talk about being betrayed and disappointed by life. Their lives are all mixed up and complicated by silly choices and stupid behavior but never the slightest hint of personal blame. I sometimes want to cry out to these people, "For heaven's sake, what else can you expect if you live like this? If you want to find life, then listen to Jesus and obey him." But you will read a long time before finding a modern novel picturing people in any other guise than victims.

Or you may turn to the psychological interpretation of life, and I think that if this discipline has done many things for us, it has done many things to us. It has a tendency to imply that moral failure is sickness and that nobody actually sins but only gets ill. Of course, we must agree that this is oftentimes true of men who are grappling with powers beyond themselves. But one of the most dangerous ideas ever to gain popularity is that moral failure is only illness and entails no personal responsibility. The alcoholic is never willing to remember that there was a time when he could choose and he chose the wrong way in spite of the warnings of parents and friends. Finally, we assume that everybody is free of blame and nobody is responsible for anything.

The sociologist makes his contribution to this general mood. If it was not our parents' fault, then it is the city's fault or the country's failure. We see ourselves as the victims of social forces beyond our control, and they mold us to their own desire. Society becomes the enemy as the person loses himself in the mass.

It is refreshing to look at a young man who believes there is a good life which he has missed. I am sure that he had stood in the crowds more than once and listened to the Galilean teacher. Jesus impressed him as having what he knew he wanted and must find. He had listened to this prophet from Nazareth speak, and the words carried authority and hope. So there came a time when he could wait no longer and ran to hear the secret. He knew he must do something about it, and there was no profit in bewailing the sadness of his life and wallowing in his despair. There was someone who could tell him what he needed to do and he must go to him quickly.

He asked, What shall I do? There is a sense, of course, in which he was quite wrong because the good life is not mere busyness. It is being. We shall never find it by doing or by obeying the Commandments. But he was quite right in recognizing that nothing could happen until he made the choice and opened up his heart. It is true that there is always something we have to do before we can find life.

There was a secretary who was never on time, and it finally exhausted her employer's patience. She came in late one morning and he said severely, "You should have been here at nine o'clock." She replied, "Why? What happened?" Well, if something is going to happen to us, we shall have to be ready. Life will not meet our convenience nor seek us out, until we have decided to make a first move. This is one of the great lessons the young man has to teach us.

The last thing to note is that Jesus said

Men Must Lose To Win.

It is the paradoxical nature of life that the young man could not accept. This is no general teaching that all wealth has to be sacrificed but a specific word to a specific young man who found that his possessions stood in the way of finding what he sought.

The first impression of the Christian life is always sacrifice. Jesus goes out of his way to make clear that there is a cross in every life. He speaks of the joyful life but never of life that is cheap or easy. Often this frightens us away as it did the young man. We are likely to ask if it is not possible for us to make a deal with him. We are willing to give him this much but not everything. To this, he makes no answer and he will not bargain. There is no giving part of ourselves and withholding something for our own purposes.

Sometimes we suggest that maybe we will go part way with him, but not all the way. Again, there is no reply. His way is everything or nothing. It demands all that we have, or we can have none of his gift. And so, if it is not our possessions, then it will be something else we want to hold onto, and even after we seek him out, we may still turn away sorrowful.

But we have to believe that what we will receive is well worth anything that it costs. If the young man could have understood how Jesus loved him and how it was out of this love that he gave his command, he could have been saved. It is for us to believe that God puts His demands upon us not because He wants to make us squirm but because He wants to help us live.

There is an old legend that later on this young man came back to Jesus. He had thought it all over and decided that he ought to do what was commanded of him, and he did it. He is the one, according to the legend, who became the Beloved Disciple. I like that legend and I think it may be true. Perhaps the story had a happy ending after all.

Arthur Miller, one of our outstanding playwrights, was discussing the stage and what makes a drama great. He said that in any successful play there must be something which makes the audience say within themselves, "My God—that's me." Well, here is a great drama, and if we look at that young man and say within our hearts, "That's me," it will have done its work. Then we will know what we must do to receive eternal life which he came to give to all who are willing to ask for it and able to receive it.

One Witness in One World

He is before all things, and in him all things hold together."   COLOSSIANS 1:17

THOSE ARE among the most audacious words I have ever read, for Paul was speaking about a person who was at the time known by a very few people. Yet he dares to announce that in Jesus Christ, God has given the world someone to prevent it from flying apart. Sometime during the second century another Christian said essentially the same thing about Christians. We do not know his name, but he wrote a letter to a friend which has come down to us as "The Epistle to Diognetus." In that letter he talked about Christians being the soul of the world, and he said that "they hold the world together."

Today in the twentieth century when the Church is stronger and Christians much more numerous, we do not seem to have this same faith. More times than we would like to admit, Christians have been at war with one another. Instead of being a part of the healing of our divisions, they have sometimes caused them. Today we begin to think of our world and the significance of the Christian faith in such a world. We must rise above our pettiness and look at our faith as Paul saw it.

The first thing I want to suggest to you is that we live in

One World.

One could hardly think of a more trite phrase, but I remember when it was not trite. In 1943 Wendell Willkie, the defeated Republican candidate for the presidency, wrote a book with this same title. It was an exciting idea at that time, and it took courage and faith to announce it in the midst of the most terrible war men had experienced. For the book was the story of a flight around the world on a military plane and a report of interviews with political and military leaders of many nations. Willkie said that in spite of the war, every man's destiny was now bound up with every other man in the world.

This has become commonplace to us, and we are aware of how small this globe has become. In the 1500's man sailed around the world in a wooden sailing ship and it took nearly three years. In the middle of the nineteenth century he went around the world in a steel motor-driven ship and it took him about three months. In the late 1930's he flew around the world in an aluminum airplane in about three days. In our time we have seen man orbit the world in about an hour. The end is not yet.

When George Washington was inaugurated President it took almost two days for the news to reach Philadelphia from New York, and it took six weeks for the news to reach Paris. Now almost any happening anywhere is known everywhere else in a matter of a few seconds.

In the autumn of 1964 we flew from Tel-Aviv to New York in a day after stopping at Paris and London en route. It was a rather long day, it is true, but such journeys are now commonplace. One of my laymen who is president of Lockheed told me that we are at the beginning. Already plans are made for air liners traveling at over two thousand miles an hour at 70,000 feet elevation.

If the world has grown smaller, it has grown more and more the same. In 1935 I went on a bicycle trip through Europe. There were very few cars on the highways, and the main hazard was the five o'clock rush in cities like Copenhagen where the streets were filled with people hurrying home from work on their bicycles. In 1960 my wife and I went to Europe, bought a car and traveled around over the Continent. I do not think we will do it again because the trucks and heavy traffic made us think of the Hollywood Freeway at five o'clock, which is no vision of Paradise.

It becomes more difficult each year to tell much difference between European capitals so far as styles and customs of the people are concerned. Some people call this the Americanization of the world, but it is probably the industrialization of the world where more and more we become like one another in the way we dress, the ways we make a living, and the way we live.

In 1951 when we were in Israel, we heard about the Yemenite Jews being flown to Israel from a country that was still living in the twelfth century. What would it do to people from the Middle Ages to be carried suddenly into the twentieth century by an airplane? It was not as catastrophic as some had feared. The Yemenite Jews said it was a fulfillment of a prophecy in Exodus that He would bear them up on eagles' wings. Yet those people sat on the floor in a Tel-Aviv bus because they did not know the purpose of benches. A few years ago I sat on the terrace of a hotel in Tiberius on the shore of the Lake of Galilee. I tried to imagine the scene when Jesus a man from Nazareth walked the shores, preached, and enlisted disciples. I was doing pretty well until an ungodly noise from the water broke up my reverie. A power boat roared across the lake, pulling a water skier. I might as well have been at Newport or Laguna Beach.

Some people resent anybody outside the country making any comment or expressing an opinion on American political affairs. But our elections have crucial implications for people all over the world even as any economic policy we adopt affects the livelihood and the welfare of families on the other side of the world. It is not possible any longer for any nation to say that it can run its affairs without other people being affected and therefore expressing a concern. Their lives are at stake. We are one population and we are one world.

Some time ago Secretary of State Rusk got off a plane in Geneva to attend an international conference. He was met at the plane by his British counterpart, and the Secretary asked, "How are we doing?" The Englishman replied, "We're keeping our fingers crossed." Which is a fairly good description of the situation. It is one world with its fingers crossed.

Now the second thing I want to say is that the one world is also

One Mess.

This has been a great disappointment to us, for we have thought rather naïvely that such a world would result inevitably in a good world. We forgot that some of the most bitter quarrels take place between neighbors, and some of our main problems arise because people live too close together. So we find ourselves with the space barriers down but no unity of heart and mind. A Swiss Protestant psychiatrist, Dr. Paul Tournier, wrote a book with the intriguing title *The Whole Person in a Broken World*. It is noteworthy that at the very time when the world seems to be one, persons seem to be broken.

The situation is symbolized for us by the Berlin Wall. Here is a great city divided by two nations, two ideologies, two sets of values. How ridiculous that in a day like ours we should have a wall separating East Berlin from West Berlin, incidentally to keep them in rather than to keep us out. People have risked their lives to escape from the East, and many have been killed in the attempt.

We spent an evening in October, 1964, with David Ben-Gurion, the long-time Prime Minister of Israel and one of its founders. I shall not forget that when I asked about the future, he grew quiet and thoughtful. He reminded me that they were two and a half million people surrounded by over forty million Arabs who had sworn to drive the Jews into the sea and destroy them. One world, indeed! I had been on the other side and visited the Arab refugees who have been driven from their homes and have lived in poverty and squalor for more than a decade.

In our own country we are in the midst of a revolution. One-tenth of our population has arisen to claim what the Constitution promised all Americans from the beginning. For a hundred years our Negro brethren have been patient and now the patience is at an end. We saw violence flare during a long hot summer and there will be more of it. Their victory is sure and this will be a better America. In the meantime, we are a divided people and we have trouble.

We live in a time of extremism both on the left and particularly on the right. It is a period of nostalgia when a considerable portion of our people think it is possible to go backward and create an isolated society which can be selfish and irresponsible. The bitter, uncharitable, unforgiving spirit of Hitler, Mussolini, and McCarthy is ever with us.

We must be concerned with the growing instability among people. Mental disease is increasing and the psychiatric wards of hospitals are full to overflowing. Surely, it is something to worry about that in our time individuals feel less secure and more threatened than ever before. Dr. Jung said that neurotic people are all searching for religion, and that is a commentary on the state of our Christianity.

On the night of March 13, 1964, a young woman, Miss Catherine Genovese, was stabbed to death on Austin Street in Queens, New York City. A. M. Rosenthal of *The New York Times* wrote a little book about the tragedy, which he called *Thirty-eight Witnesses*. There were thirty-eight different people who heard her cry for help and did not even call the police. They were not bad people, but each one said that he did not want to get involved. Rosenthal said, "I always thought that if I wrote a book, it would be about India or Poland or Africa or some other faraway place I've spent some time in, but here I end up writing about Austin Street in Queens." There was One who nearly two thousand years ago told about a man going down from Jerusalem to Jericho who fell among robbers. But there was a Samaritan who came by and helped him. What kind of a story would he tell about a young woman killed in the midst of a great city? What was it that Edmund Burke wrote so long ago? He said that all that was necessary for the triumph of evil was that good men do nothing.

I read about a circus lion escaping from his cage in a European town. Everyone was excited and afraid and they were warned to stay inside and bolt the doors until the lion was found. They found him all right, cowering in a barn. He had done no harm to anyone except himself. He was on the verge of what in human beings is called a nervous breakdown. If he could have talked, he would have said that modern life was too much for him. It reminded me that George Bernard Shaw said he could never admire a lion tamer's courage, because when he was in the cage with the lions, at least people could not get to him. People scared him and they scare me. We live in one world and we live in one mess.

The third thing I want to say is the good news that we have

One Faith.

We are not going to be united by business. The fact that the Russians use the same kind of tractors we use does not bring us closer together. The building of smooth highways and the selling of more cars does not create unity. The manufacture of the same machines does not destroy prejudice or hatred. It does not create sympathy and mutual concern.

We shall not be united by science. When the Russians made an atomic bomb in a much shorter space than we thought was possible, it frightened us. When France exploded an atomic warhead, we did not feel this meant progress. Now that Red China has joined the atom club, we know that our danger has increased immeasurably. Dr. Harold Urey, one of our leading scientists, confessed he was scared and that all the scientists he knew were scared.

Our only hope is a common faith in God and a sense of common destiny. The great thing about the ecumenical situation today is that we are aware of our oneness in a way that has not been true for a long time. The Vatican Council has shown our Roman Catholic brethren in a more receptive mood. They refer to us as "separated brethren" and not as heretics bound for hell. That is good. Protestant groups are moving toward minimizing their differences and appreciating the things they have in common. It is a great thing that today we are beginning to realize that there is much more to hold us together than there is to separate us, and the tide moves in the direction of unity.

Some time ago, I was invited to speak at an organization meeting for a new council of churches in a Los Angeles suburb. To my surprise and delight, the Roman Catholic priest attended. He came up afterward and I said to him, "Father, I wish I could find words to tell you how glad I am to have you here." The young man not long out of seminary said, "Bishop, we have longed for Christian fellowship with you as much as you have with us." I am seeing things happening in Catholic-Protestant relations I never expected to see in my lifetime.

Paul saw this oneness so clearly he dared to announce that Christ is the One who holds the world together. The writer of the Epistle to Dognetus saw it so clearly he dared to affirm that the Christians' high calling is to hold the world together. Today it becomes more apparent than ever before that in God alone is our hope of brotherhood, and Christians are bearing witness to it.

This is not just the word of a preacher. Arnold Toynbee wrote an article recently for the *Saturday Review* fortieth anniversary number in which he said religion was our hope for the future. It is the wisdom of the great religions which will save us from disaster, he said. I heard him lecture more than a decade ago and thought I had never heard anyone who sounded more like God. He was not disturbed by the morning headlines but gave us the long look. In great religion is the answer to our cry for hope, but he summed it all up by quoting from St. John's First Epistle: "Let us love one another; for love is of God; and every one that loveth is born of God, and knoweth God" (4:7, AV). Remember how Bertrand Russell some time ago rather apologetically announced that the answer to our problems was in what the Christians call "love." Quite a testimony from great scholars!

Years ago when Mayor Hylan of New York was making many speeches, he sometimes had to deliver one that was written for him but not read by him. On one such occasion the writer had put in a joke which struck the mayor as so funny that he burst out laughing and his eyeglasses fell off and splintered on the floor. The chairman of the meeting had to finish the speech for him. There are Christians who are coming face to face in our day for the first time with the height, the depth, and the breadth of their faith and it fills them with joy. It comes as a great surprise that in Christ we are united to all men and all nations and all classes. In spite of differences of litany and theology and tradition, in the one world there is one faith.

Finally, there is

One Answer.

G. K. Chesterton said one time that nothing is real until it is local. We ask ourselves where we are going to start, and the answer is so simple that it frightens us. We are going to start right where we are in our local church.

I can think of a good many people who will say that this tremendous task can never begin in the local church which is too petty and full of bickering. It can quarrel over little things and turn itself into a second-rate club made up of people with small courage and no vision. All of us who have worked in churches know the things that can be said against them. But Paul knew something about this when he wrote to those early Christians. Read over again his letter to the Corinthians who were, if it is possible, much worse than we are.

What we must do is receive the vision of what the Church is called upon to be in our time. It is a great thing for us to be reminded that the answer to the divided world is Christ. It is a startling thing to be aware suddenly that the Church is his body. Perhaps what Christendom needs now more than anything else is to have its people baptized with a new vision of what the Church is. We need to realize who we are.

When we do this we shall have a word for all the world. Somebody once wrote to the editor of a little newspaper in Maine that his items were so local they were universal. Once we get the thing clear in our mind again, we will know that God calls ordinary people to preach and demonstrate His power and His desire to save us from destroying ourselves.

When I was in Jordan and Israel, I went to Bethlehem where Jesus was born and to Nazareth where he was brought up. I stood beside the Well of Sychar where he talked to a woman long ago and changed her life. I went up to Jerusalem as he did as a boy and later to be crucified. And I thought to myself, "How small is this land and how far it was from the center of things." You can drive all over it in a few hours, and he spent his whole life here. Was it God's plan to save the world with one solitary life in this small country? Paul said it was and two thousand years of history say it was.

So we may believe in that fellowship called the Church as the instrument of His saving grace. It contains the power of God. It is as Radhakrishnan of India said in derision, ordinary people making extraordinary claims. It is the answer to the world's need for something to hold it together.

A long time ago as a student, I read Saint-Exupéry's book *Wind, Sand and Stars*. He was a French aviator who wrote beautifully about flying and life. I read practically everything he wrote and found him full of inspiration and wisdom. He was recalled to military service in World War II and was flying an observation mission without any guns in his plane on July 31, 1944. He was shot down by a young German who was writing a doctoral thesis on the work of Saint-Exupéry and who had come to admire him as a great writer and a great man. When he learned whom he had destroyed, he went to pieces and was sent to a psychiatric hospital. All he could say was, "I killed my master." In that story there is the tragedy of our time. We kill what we love, and we destroy ourselves when we kill our brothers. The Christian church must awaken us to the truth of our oneness in God and proclaim that through Christ we are healed. It is one world in one mess and God has given us the one answer in our Christian faith made real by the Christian churches.